Whitetail Success

Hunting Hard, Hunting Smart

Hunting Wisdom Library™

NORTH★AMERICAN★HUNTING★CLUB

MINNETONKA, MINNESOTA

About the Author

Gregg Gutschow hit the Wisconsin whitetail woods at age 12 and hasn't stopped since. As editor of *North American Hunter* magazine, Gregg's whitetail hunting adventures now take him to all points of the compass, in addition to the northwoods and farmland deer haunts he grew up with. His message for deer hunting success is simple, and it applies no matter where you pursue whitetails, how you go about it, or how long you've been at it: Hunt hard, hunt smart.

WHITETAIL SUCCESS: HUNTING HARD, HUNTING SMART

Mike Vail
Vice President, Products and Business Development

Tom Carpenter
Director of Book and New Media Development

Dan Kennedy
Book Production Manager

Heather Koshiol
Book Development Coordinator

Dave Schelitzche
Book Design and Production

Phil Aarrestad
Commissioned Photography

Matt Preis
Book Development Assistant

Special thanks to Paul Radde

1 2 3 4 5 6 7 8 / 02 01 00 99

ISBN 1-58159-075-X

North American Hunting Club
12301 Whitewater Drive
Minnetonka, Minnesota 55343

PHOTO CREDITS

Charles J. Alsheimer, 17, 21 (bottom), 24, 25 (right), 30, 37 (top), 48 (top), 54 (left), 54 (right), 58, 61 (top), 68, 76 (left), 77, 78, 95 (top), 101, 106, 125, 157 (top); Kenny Bahr, 12 (top), 80 (top); Mike Barlow, 10, 27 (right), 36, 98–99, 121, 127, 135, 146, 154–155; Bill Buckley/The Green Agency, 1 (left), 16 (2 bottom), 59, 113 (bottom), 130, 134 (left); Dawn Charging, 119; Judd Cooney, 1 (right), 42 (both), 49, 62 (left), 82, 86 (bottom), 91; Tim Christie, 120; Dan Dietrich, 18 (bottom), 60; Michael D. Faw, 45 (left); Tom Fegely, 52, 70, 96 (bottom), 105 (left), 126 (bottom), 133, 138; Gregg Gutschow, 13 (bottom), 157 (bottom); Brad Herndon, 13 (top), 28, 31 (bottom left), 32 (bottom), 34, 41, 64, 92, 94, 104, 110, 141, 143, 151; Carol Herndon, 139; M.R. James, 22 (left); Tes Randle Jolly, 16 (top), 23 (bottom), 63 (top), 73 (left), 81, 148; Donald M. Jones, 11, 44 (both), 48 (bottom), 50 (top), 69, 115, 116, 117, 156, 61; Mark Kayser, 46, 84, 87, 112 (bottom), 66–67, 75, 88-89, 134 (right), 137; Mitch Kezar, 22 (right), 26, 29 (bottom), 63 (bottom), 65, 76 (right), 90 (both), 105; Bill Kinney, cover onlay, 29 (top right), 31 (top), 38–39, 40, 47, 56 (bottom); Lance Krueger, 4, 29 (left), 45 (right), 97, 111, 113 (top), 132, 153; Bill Marchel, 8–9, 18 (top right), 20, 21 (top), 31 (bottom right), 35 (bottom), 43, 55, 72, 74, 83, 114, 118 (both), 149; Neal & Mary Jane Mishler, 6–7, 51 (left), 62 (right), 80 (bottom), 126 (top); Mark Raycroft, 15, 23 (top), 33, 57 (right), 71; Mike Searles, 35 (top), 79, 85, 152 (right), 109, 147; Jim Shockey, 122, 123; Dusan Smetana, 25 (left), 150; Ron Spomer, 19, 32 (top), 86 (top), 100, 108, 129, 131, 136 (top); Bill Vaznis, 14, 53, 56 (top), 73 (right), 102, 136 (bottom), 140. Thanks to Ameristep, Inc., 107, Golden Eagle/Satellite Archery, 144; Outland Sports, 93 (both), 95 (left); Underbrush, Inc., 107. Remaining photographs property of NAHC: 12 (bottom), 18 (top left), 27 (left), 37 (left), 41, 50 (bottom), 51 (right), 96 (top), 103, 129–130, 142, 145 (both).

Table of Contents

Foreword

Different deer hunters are best suited to different brands of deer hunting. There are those who can sit in a stand hour after hour, day after day, week after week yet stay as alert and attentive as on opening morning. There are those who can discern a particular buck's trail in the new snow and follow it, like a hungry wolf, to an inevitable conclusion. There are those who rely mostly on good optics and boot leather and silent clothing to spot and stalk big bucks, then shoot them in their beds. There are others whose aggressive rattling and calling styles bring the big deer to them.

When you look at the names of those hunters in the magazines and record books and see them on videotapes and television shows, you'll notice that what they have in common are results. These are the hunters who "always get their deer." What you might not notice is that they frequently rely on one primary method of hunting. If they're rattlers, they tend to be rattlers wherever they hunt. If they are still-hunters, then that's what they're likely to do in Maine or in Texas. If they are stand hunters, they can fine-tune an ambush site in a palmetto flat or a prairie province wheat field.

Rare is the deer hunter who understands fully the myriad of tactics that can be applied to whitetail hunting during the course of a season, across the deer's incredibly broad range, and from season to season. While *North American Hunter* editor Gregg Gutschow has his preferred hunting methods just like everyone else, he also has a strong grasp of all the other whitetail hunting techniques and methods ... and myths. Gregg is a rare hunter and writer indeed.

Gregg has hunted whitetails across the length and breadth of their range enough to have experienced all these hunting methods personally, but his qualifications to write for discriminating NAHC members go way beyond that. Gregg is an outstanding reporter. He meticulously seeks to back up his personal experiences and observations about deer hunting with facts from top hunters who specialize in each particular style of whitetail hunting.

The stories and factual reporting you are about to enjoy were assembled by Gregg with one goal: to help you hunt whitetails more successfully. While some tidbit of information or morsel of woods lore might not directly apply to your most common hunting situation, you can rest assured of one thing: If it's in this book, it's fact and it's documented as a proven way to take more and bigger whitetails. With this book under your belt, whatever your hunting goals, you'll be a better hunter—period.

Learn, enjoy ... and good luck with your whitetail hunting.

Best afield,

Bill

Bill Miller
Executive Director
North American Hunting Club

INTRODUCTION

s editor of *North American Hunter* magazine, I'm fortunate to have the opportunity to hunt white-tailed deer in many good places. But I'll never forget my first out-of-state deer hunt just after I broke into this business.

It was in Missouri. Jim Zumbo was there, so were Jim Shockey, Larry Weishuhn, Bill Jordan and a bunch of other deer hunters you've probably read about or seen on hunting videos.

I felt as humbled then as I've felt while writing this book. The difference is that now *I'm* on the spot. At that camp in Missouri all those years ago, I listened more than I spoke. And I didn't attempt to offer any deer hunting wisdom for those guys to take to their stands. On these pages, I'm going to attempt to do just that, for you. But I'll have help provided by some of those same hunters listed above and many others.

I've been hunting whitetails religiously for 20 years, but I'm no expert. In fact, if I traveled to your neck of the woods, I'd ask *you* where the deer feed and bed, and where the main travel corridors are. From there I might fine-tune a stand site or try a particular tactic with scents or calls; or I might spend a whole day on stand to see if the deer are moving midday. The bottom line is, there is no magic formula, no big secret about killing mature bucks, and nothing the "experts" do that you can't.

So why a book at all? What is there to hunting whitetails successfully? A lot of little things. A mountain of little things.

Many hunting writers and publications seem to think that it's necessary to wow you with "new" sure-fire techniques to take big bucks. In fact, it's my personal view that this effort has helped to erode the foundation of successful whitetail hunting. The "techno" world we live in has permeated the whitetail woods to the point where deer hunters are offered deer movement charts and other "stuff" that is supposed to eliminate "wasted" time on stand. Let me tell you something right now; if you're looking for a quick fix to your deer hunting, you'll not find it here. And if you believe that the hours on stand when no deer are in view are "wasted," you'll never become a successful deer hunter.

In this book, I'll do my level best to get back to the basics of successful whitetail hunting, while at the same time offering up all of the latest techniques and gear that you should know. I'll have met my personal goals for this book if you learn from it, whether this upcoming season is your first or 50th.

Let's go deer hunting!

Chapter 1

THE FOUNDATION

This chapter, as the title suggests, should lay the ground-work for hunting whitetails successfully. It stresses persistence and perspiration. No style points are handed out in deer hunting.

I'm glad that I didn't grow up in an area that had a lot of whitetails, and I'm glad that I didn't kill a mature buck until well into my deer hunting career. If I had early on, I might have been spoiled. I might have thought that I ought to kill a nice buck every season. And maybe, if I then faced a difficult run of two or three seasons in a row without a deer, I would have decided that deer hunting's payoffs weren't worth the investment in time.

We people in the business of communicating the hunting experience, especially on television and videos, foster an instant-gratification attitude by painting an unrealistic picture of what deer hunting is really like. You've seen the whitetail videos or hunts on TV. Deer everywhere! And, before you know it, a big buck strolls into view where the hunter makes the shot to provide another happy ending. Then it's on to the next deer hunt and another monster buck.

And then we wonder why deer hunters don't want to hear about patience and the art of sitting still and what deer hunting discipline really means. Deer hunting, too often, is portrayed in a way that less than 1 percent of the deer hunters might some day experience. For the 10 million or so deer hunters in the United States, deer hunting is 99 percent learning and 1 percent results.

In the real world, big bucks don't charge in to the sound of a grunt call or rattling antlers every time. There are probably more days when you don't see a buck than when you do. The hunter who pays attention to deer hunting's fundamentals, and then puts in as much time as he possibly can, stands the best chance of being rewarded for his effort.

That's the foundation of this chapter. I hope that you enjoy it and profit from it. And I especially hope that if you have a young up-and-coming deer hunter in the family, he or she might take stock in its message too.

PUTTING IN YOUR TIME

By this point in your deer hunting career, you've probably read about the merits of hunting whitetails all day long, and the studies about how mature bucks are often seen during midday hours. But I'll venture to guess that, despite good intentions, most of us don't stick it out all day. It's difficult even when the weather is cooperating. But when it's cold, windy or rainy, spending all day on stand becomes the ultimate test of discipline.

Maybe more important than hunting all day is hunting as many hours as you possibly can. When I first started out as a deer hunter, I kept a notebook log of how many hours I hunted from my homemade treestand and even noted the weather conditions during each hunt. I was *into* my deer hunting! My optimistic side told me that the more hours I spent in my treestand, the better my odds of killing a deer.

Looking back, I like the dedication that I showed, and time in a stand is important, but it needs to be coupled with intelligent hunting strategy. And that's where I was lacking, returning time and again to the same plywood platform and tracking human scent to the same tree over and over.

I'm sure that by the time I finally killed my first deer from that stand, all the local deer knew where the stand was located. They probably just figured that I wasn't that much of a threat since most of them had traveled by at one time or another without any consequence. Still, most of the deer that I saw were does and fawns. I saw a few small-racked bucks, but never any big ones there, despite the fact that I did see a big buck a couple of times in the adjacent alfalfa field. I couldn't understand why he didn't come by my stand if some of the other deer were. Big bucks, I eventually learned, were different animals. And while putting in your time is important, it's not enough.

TIME VS. GEAR

But, if I had two hunters of equal ability and could move them to a number of different stands, depending on wind direction and deer movement, and one of the hunters had the aid of all the scents and calls on the market and the other hunter had twice the amount of time to hunt but none of the scents or calls, I'd bet my money on the guy who puts in the extra time over the guy relying on the gear. The foundation of hunting whitetails successfully is discipline and time on-stand coupled with smart strategy.

Let's look at it another way. Take two deer hunters. One uses a game movement chart and hunts the days when the chart says that his odds of seeing deer are above average. Say that there are 25 such days during a typical 100-day season including gun, bow and special seasons. Now take a second hunter who hunts the other 75 days that the chart says will be average or below average deer movement days. Which guy do I bet on? You got it, the guy who puts in three times as many hours.

JUST HUNT

Sure, deer have tendencies just like we do. They might move more when the winds are less than 25 mph. They might move less during periods of heavy rain or snow. Or

Deer hunters who hunt long and hard, and pay attention to their surroundings stand the best odds of consistent success.

Whitetails can be up and moving during most any weather conditions. Hunt smart, and don't let inclement weather scare you off.

maybe you'll pin your hopes on a barometer moving one way or the other. I say this: Just hunt. Hunt whenever you possibly can and play whatever hand the weather deals you. Maybe you notice that the deer seem to hit the fields during a light rain. Maybe you've seen them bed on a south-facing slope when it gets extremely cold.

I've seen deer on their feet under almost every conceivable type of weather. Now, I'm happier some mornings than others when I look outside at the weather, but it has to be pretty extreme to convince me that I have no chance of taking a deer.

SUCCESS IN THE WIND

A few years ago in late October a friend and I traveled to a southern Minnesota farm for a long weekend of bowhunting. It was abnormally cold, something like 15°F for daytime highs, as I recall. But the wind was the real killer. Our first morning out it must have been blowing 25 mph. The guy on the radio said that it was minus 20° or 30°F with the wind chill. I survived for a few hours on stand that morning, but I didn't see a deer and figured we wouldn't do any good until the wind quit. Early afternoon we were headed back out to the farm and saw a young buck chase a doe across the road right in front of the truck. The wind was still howling in excess of 20 mph, but my friend and I looked at each other

with some hope for the afternoon hunt.

Less than an hour after climbing into my treestand, I saw my first deer, a doe, but she turned off the trail heading toward my stand and disappeared. A flock of turkeys worked the ridge right behind my stand, yelping and kee-keeing, but I could barely hear them above the wind. Moments after the doe disappeared, a 1½-year-old 8-point buck appeared on the same trail on which the doe had been walking toward my

The author withstood 30 mph winds and abnormally cold October weather to take this 208-pound southern Minnesota buck.

stand. But he must have been able to follow her foot-scent, and he too veered off and out of sight.

Not five minutes after that, I saw a huge-bodied buck step out in the exact same spot. His 8-point rack was wide, but not high or particularly massive. His body size is what impressed me, and I immediately decided that if I got the chance, I'd shoot. The buck hit the intersection where the doe and young buck had peeled off and stopped. Two scrapes were ahead of him on the trail and within bow range of my stand. I hoped that he'd choose to work the scrapes instead of following the deer that had gone the other direction. He did!

Five excruciating minutes later, after watching the buck paw each of the two scrapes, he gave me a perfect broadside shot at 17 yards. My arrow sliced his heart. After the buck disappeared from sight, mortally wounded, the sound of the howling wind and the sensation of my swaying treestand returned. Had I looked out my front door at those weather conditions, I would have been inclined to wait for tomorrow. But because I hunted, I notched my tag on a buck that field dressed at 208 pounds.

SUCCESS IN THE SNOW

Another hunt stands out in my mind. It was opening day of the Wisconsin firearms deer season, and the northeastern part of the state, where our camp is located, had been blanketed by 10 inches of heavy snow overnight. Despite the risk of getting stuck on the treacherous deep-woods logging roads, we locked in the four-wheel drive and bulled our way miles into our hunting area.

Less than an hour after first light, my friend, Pat, one of the original members of our deer camp, killed the best buck he's ever taken in his life. In fact, that 16-inch-wide 7-point is the second-best buck ever to come from our northwoods deer

Despite a 10-inch snowfall overnight, this northern Wisconsin buck was up and moving early on opening day of the rifle season.

camp, where antler development is generally not good because of poor forage and severe winters.

And despite the nearly knee-deep snow, most of us saw as many or more deer than on an average opener. With almost nonexistent hunting pressure in our area, the deer sightings that day can't be attributed to movement resulting from deer being pushed by other hunters. So much for the first big snowfall hampering deer movement.

Having the proper gear and supplies will help you hunt longer hours in comfort.

YOU CAN'T PREDICT "WHEN"

A friend and I used to seriously "hunt" muskies, "the fish of 10,000 casts" as they're popularly known in the Upper Midwest. Though we paid attention to weather and bait selection and lake structure, we boiled down muskie fishing success to "time on the water." Just about the time you figured there wasn't another muskie left in the lake, one would charge from the depths and smash your lure, just as you were about to pull it from the water and go home.

Here is the bottom line: deer don't have any schedule to follow. Despite our best efforts to decipher deer travel patterns and times, we sometimes see deer, including mature bucks, when and where we least expect to see them. Some of the most dedicated deer biologists working in the field have spent years trying to solve all the mysteries that determine deer behavior. We have a few answers from all of that research, but not nearly enough to predict deer movement with any reliable accuracy. Deer are wild, unpredictable animals. And I, for one, like it that way.

That being the case, I say hunt whenever you possibly can from opening day until closing. Don't put all your chips on the rut. Don't take the view that deer won't move when it's windy. Don't think that all the big bucks were shot or run out of the area during the regular firearms season. They're still there, and as the old saying goes, "You can't kill a deer if you're sitting in camp."

DEER HUNTING DISCIPLINE

I remember receiving a copy of *The Archer's Bible* by Fred Bear for Christmas my eleventh year. I can't tell you everything that this budding bowhunter found in that wonderful book, but I can tell you that I have always carried some of Fred's words with me to my deer stand. And as I began to write this book, I dusted off *The Archer's Bible* and turned again to those pages that I had read over so many times in my youth. Here is one excerpt that jumped out at me again.

"Many hunters believe they are being quiet in a blind, when actually they are turning and twisting about in a continual effort to watch all directions where game might appear," Fred wrote. "Alertness is necessary, but it should not be exercised at the expense of quietness. Any movement, such as turning the head, should be made slowly and deliberately. Remember that it is movement the game detects most easily."

FOLLOWING FRED'S WISDOM

For whatever reason, this information hit me like a hammer. It made sense, even way back then. When I turned 12, I ventured to the deer woods for the first time with a Bear Kodiak compound bow in my hand and a real Wisconsin deer tag in my pocket. I think I wanted a deer more than anything else a 12-year-old boy could ever want. So I had no problem obeying Fred's words.

And it didn't take me long to realize that Fred was right. I wore faded woodland camo and no scent-control suit. I stood on a plywood platform nailed in the middle of a triple-trunked maple, not 10 feet off the ground. I hunted that same stand no matter which direction the wind blew. And despite it all, I saw deer almost every time I hunted. And only a handful of them ever saw me—because I stood still, painfully still.

Young joints and muscles allowed it physically, but Fred's words provided the mental discipline. In fact, I was so driven to prevent a deer from seeing me that I refused to move at all if I heard a twig snap or leaves crunch behind me. I reasoned that I'd never get turned 180 degrees without the deer seeing me anyway, so why risk spooking it? Better to be patient and let it walk by me and out front where I could simply raise my bow, draw and shoot.

THE REWARDS OF DISCIPLINE & PATIENCE

In hindsight, I still think that this approach was wise for a young bowhunter with a maximum effective range of 20

You call the shot. Though some gun hunters might cleanly be able to harvest this buck, exercising descipline in your shot selection improves your odds of going home happy. It will mean that some opportunities will pass without a shot, but it will also reduce your chances of losing a wounded deer.

yards, hunting maybe 8 feet off the ground from a stand with very little surrounding cover. Yet my first shot from that stand did not come until my third season. The doe walked in, totally unaware, right below me, and the arrow hit her square in the back between the shoulders and penetrated through her lungs. Three years of bowhunting. One shot. One deer that died within 70 yards of my stand.

My percentage more than 15 years later is no longer 100 percent. I've missed some and I've hit a couple other deer that I failed to recover. And though some of these mistakes are simply part of the bowhunting game, others I'll chalk up to lapses in the discipline that Fred harped about in his book.

Today my bow is much faster than that old Bear Kodiak. I wear better camo patterns and pay closer attention to the wind. I move stand locations and nestle small portable stands 20 to 25 feet off the ground in places where I have good surrounding cover to break up my outline. Taken individually, these are improvements to how I hunt whitetails today, compared to when I started. Yet I've sometimes believed that these tactics would help me get away with more movement or try a less-than-perfect-shot opportunity. And you know

what? Most times when I've ignored that strict discipline Fred preached, I've regretted it.

I've had whitetails spot me despite exceptionally high stands and carefully chosen camouflage. I've moved to take shots that probably would have become better shots if I'd been a bit more patient.

To Native Americans, the hunt was an extremely spiritual event. So much so that they believed a deer communicated to the hunter by a long stare, when it was ready to allow the hunter to take its life. The hunter who lacked the discipline, patience and respect to wait for the signal from the animal failed to take the deer. Whether or not you believe that this type of reverence is necessary to become a successful deer hunter, there is a great deal to be said for the importance of discipline.

DISCIPLINED PREPARATION

I've been on deer hunts where I've heard other hunters say that they just didn't have time to sight-in their rifle or get their bow perfectly tuned. I've also spoken to outfitters who

Concentrated practice leads to concentrated shooting afield. Consider every shot—whether it's in practice or not—your one and only shot.

have lamented about hunters, some of whom spend thousands of dollars for a five-day hunt, who arrive in camp ill-prepared to take a deer. And these aren't always beginning hunters who don't know any better. Quite often veteran hunters just figure that because they've killed enough deer with a particular rifle or bow, they don't need to practice any more. Or they figure that sitting in a stand isn't physically demanding, so they don't have to get in shape.

On a recent Western whitetail hunt, I watched in horror as a couple of new hunters in camp cleanly missed a 3-D archery target from 20 yards. And they missed it repeatedly as their arrows flew sloppily from bows that were badly out of tune. Needless to say, they didn't fare well out in the field. I think the outfitter would have liked to have given their money back and sent them home.

Not only are your odds of success decreased if you go afield unprepared, your odds of wounding and losing a whitetail are dramatically increased. And that's unethical. We can't control the buck-to-doe ratio of the local deer herd, the timing of the rut or the weather, but we can control our equipment and our bodies. And if you want to consistently be successful as a deer hunter, I can't think of any better way than to start right here. Control the controllable.

SHOOT AS OFTEN AS YOU CAN

I'll get into the specifics of bow-shooting and rifle-shooting preparation later in this book, but suffice it to say that you should shoot as often as possible. You'll be ready when drawing your bow or shouldering your rifle becomes so automatic that the thought process isn't even necessary, it just happens at the right time. You center the crosshairs or sight pin and squeeze the trigger or release the bowstring the same way you've done hundreds, maybe thousands, of times at the range.

Living in the North, I generally don't do much shooting from January through March. But once the snow melts and the weather warms in April, I start shooting my bow at least once a week. Come June and July, I'm shooting every other day until bow season opens in September. And even during the season I try to shoot a couple arrows every other day to stay sharp.

I don't think that my practice regimen is extreme. In fact, I usually feel like I should be shooting even more. Bowhunting requires a great deal of hand-eye coordination. I find that it's like playing golf—the more I play, the better I play. And if I'm shooting my bow well on the prac-

Once a rifle is sighted-in, it doesn't require the everyday practice that a bow does. Still, gun hunters can improve their shooting skills by target shooting away from the bench later on. The more you shoot, the more automatic and accurate your shooting becomes.

tice range, I take a great deal of confidence with me to my treestand. That translates into more mental discipline to sit still and hunt longer; I don't have any worries about making the shot when it happens.

TUNE YOUR BODY

Sitting still and spending long hours in a treestand might not sound physically demanding, but try it sometime. In addition to the mental concentration required, the deer hunter who gets his body in tune prior to the season is able to hunt more comfortably and, therefore, more effectively. Granted, a whitetail hunt is no mountain goat hunt. But if you smoke or are over-weight or just plain out of shape, a short hike up the oak ridge can have you winded and breaking a sweat. Sweat means human odor, and *that* means that any down-wind whitetail is going to bust you before you ever get a chance to lay eyes on it. Plus, if you're in good shape, muscles won't cramp as quick-ly on stand and you'll be able to climb into your stand more safely. Most veteran deer hunters have learned that moving stands is one of the most effective ways to stay one step ahead of the deer. But hanging treestands is work. If you're in good physical condition, you'll proba-bly be more aggressive in moving stand loca-tions as dictated by deer movements and that, too, will translate into better odds of notching your tag.

Hunters in good physi-cal condition don't hesitate to move stands and hike the next ridge.

DISCIPLINE ON STAND

Sit still. Sounds simple, but I see very few deer hunters who do it really well. What do you do when a mosquito lands on your cheek during prime time late in the afternoon? Do you swat it with a quick slap, slowly raise your hand and squash it on your cheek, or let it finish sucking blood and buzz away unscathed?

I hate mosquitos as much as the next deer hunter, but I've let hundreds of them fly off unharmed carrying an abdomen-load of my blood. If I see or think that I hear a deer, I ignore the discomfort of a mosquito bite. Even if I don't hear or see anything, I'll move my hand in super-slow motion to kill the bloodsucker. It sounds like a little thing, an unimportant thing compared to other aspects of deer hunting, but I believe that deer harvest success rates would be a lot high-er across the country if more deer hunters had the discipline to sit extremely still.

Look at it like this. A white-tail's eye is best suited to detect movement. The reason is simple. If the deer sees a coyote or wolf or mountain lion move before that predator gets within striking distance, the deer survives. And sur-vival is what it's all about in the world of the whitetail. Every moment that I'm in a deer stand I try to tell myself that there's probably a deer very close; probably just out of my field of view. After all, across much of the animal's range, the whitetail lives most of its life within a one-square-mile area. So they're never that far off. If I'm shifting about in my stand or swatting a bug, or turning my head quickly side to side to scan the woods, that deer might see me first. And if it does, I have no chance to take that deer with a bow and little chance with a rifle.

Your aim is to see or hear whitetails before they see you. And since they see movement far better than detail or color, you are far better off wearing head-to-toe blaze orange in the woods and sitting perfectly still than wearing full camo and moving about constantly in your stand.

Sitting Still Made Easier

Thankfully, as we hunters get older, we get wiser and find ways to improve the comfort level of our whitetail stands.

Sure, there are excesses; like those palatial tower stands complete with recliners, heater, sliding shooting windows ... the works. These might be too comfortable and alert nearby deer when the snoring begins echoing inside the box.

On the other end of the comfort spectrum is that old treestand that I started out in, back when I was 12. It had no seat. It had no carpet over the plywood platform. I stood for as long as I could stand completely still,

Extra padding on your seat improves comfort. That means less movement and more time on stand.

sometimes two hours, sometimes four, and then I went home. A 12-year-old after his first deer can deal with a lot of discomfort.

Today I like stands with seats high enough to keep my knees flexed at a comfortable 90-degree angle. This keeps my legs from cramping and promotes better circulation, which helps keep me from getting cold. I like wide, soft padded seats so I don't get a sore butt or back. And since most of the portable treestands I like don't come with enough padding to suit me, I often carry along a cushion from one of my

Eating and drinking on stand require movement, but it's better than leaving your stand and going back to camp.

turkey hunting vests to improve the comfort factor.

I also make sure that when I set the stand I saw off limbs or anything else on the trunk that might jab me in the back while I'm trying to concentrate on deer hunting. You can't sit still if you have to sit off to the side to avoid a limb that's not cut flush to the trunk.

And with safety and comfort both in mind, I make sure that

Seat height is important on treestands. Find the seat height that promotes good circulation and doesn't cramp muscles.

the platform of my stand is positioned level to the ground. If it's leaning back or tilting toward the ground, my legs are going to cramp and I'm not going to be as safe when I get in or out of the stand, or when I stand up to shoot.

From there it's a matter of dressing properly and taking along the supplies I need to keep me comfortable. I can sit still if I'm a bit overdressed, but I can't sit very still if I'm cold. So at minimum, I always have extra gloves, stocking cap and neck warmer in my daypack. Also in the pack are some snacks and fluids to keep my stomach from urging me out of my treestand and home for lunch. I know—eating and drinking on stand means movement. But I work fast, and then I'm good for hours longer than if I hadn't brought food or drink with me.

Some hunters get bored and find that a paperback book keeps them on stand longer. I've taken a book along while hunting for pronghorns out of a blind near a waterhole, but I don't like the idea of a book in a whitetail stand: Turning pages creates too much movement, and it's also too important to keep your eyes on your surroundings. The minute you look away to find out if the butler did it is the minute a buck will appear. Now how do you get the book out of your hands and your bow or gun in your hands without him seeing you?

My friend Will Primos said something in an article in *North American Hunter* once that I'll never forget. Talking about turkey hunting, Will was asked, "What is the most effective technique you've learned to kill a turkey?" His response was one word, "Patience." The next question was, "Any advice on how to develop that attribute?" His answer was, "Learn to enjoy your surroundings."

Simple answers like that go to the core of hunting whitetails successfully.

Important Tools: Sight & Sound

When we deer hunters wait on stand, sight and sound are our advantages. We know where to look for the deer; the deer shouldn't even know that we are in the woods. We have our feet on a quiet platform or bare ground, while the deer are moving about on crunchy leaves or twigs. And research has shown that whitetails probably hear little better than we humans. So if we're disciplined on stand, we should see and hear a deer before it sees or hears us.

The deer's sense of smell, of course, is another matter, one we'll discuss at length in other chapters. Once we've settled into our stand, there's not much we can do about scent. So, again, control the controllable.

A couple seasons ago at my family's deer camp, I was sitting in my treestand when I heard a bunch of chickadees flitting through the forest from tree trunk to tree trunk, heading in my direction. I figured I'd sit statue-still to see how close one of the birds would get. Moments later one landed on the trunk of a tree a few feet away, looked about, then flew and perched on my rifle barrel. It made one jump to the rifle's receiver, then to my wrist, then to my shoulder. I rolled my eyeballs toward the bird, and I swear that it wasn't until that moment that the chickadee realized I wasn't part of the tree trunk. I've also had squirrels and other critters close enough to touch while deer hunting. Deer too, for that matter, have been nearly within arm's reach. If you've experienced the same, chances are you're doing a good job of being disciplined on stand.

Discipline at the Moment of Truth

Life in the whitetail woods should go on around you as if you're not even there; that way, the whitetails won't realize it until it's too late. But that moment too, the moment of truth, requires the utmost discipline.

Be a statue on stand. Sitting still seems like a minor detail, but few deer hunters do it really well.

You can do everything right in your preparation, your stand selection and your discipline on stand, and then blow it by not choosing your shot wisely. It doesn't matter if you're hunting with a bow or gun.

Every hunting tool and every hunter has an effective range. You have to know how far you can consistently group arrows in an 8-inch circle and how far you've practiced with your rifle. You have to know that even your state-of-the-art slug gun is a 100-yard hunting tool. You must understand shot angles and deer anatomy and be able to differentiate a high-percentage opportunity from a low-percentage one. These are restrictions that you must put on yourself and never stretch. Even when you think that no one is watching, all deer hunters are depending on your performance afield because it reflects, ultimately, on all of us. You will make mistakes. We all do. Physical mistakes, like failing to squeeze the trigger properly, happen. It is the mental errors in judgment that we must all do our best to control. The white-tailed deer deserves our respect every step of the way.

WHAT DO WE REALLY KNOW ABOUT WHITETAILS?

I f you've been deer hunting for any length of time you've undoubtedly heard things like: "A whitetail will always bed on the downwind side of a ridge with its back into the wind." Or, "A buck makes a scrape and then comes back some time later to see if a doe has urinated in it to tell that buck that she's ready to be bred."

We humans like pat answers to things, and wouldn't it be nice if we had some pat answers to white-tailed deer hunting? Sure, there are some consistencies, but "expect the unexpected" might be one of the best descriptions of what you'll find when you enter the deer woods.

I remember a couple of years ago when a friend of mine called to tell me excitedly about a Texas bowhunt he was planning for that coming October. "The outfitter said it would be prime time for rattling and that we'd rattle in 10 to 20 bucks a day," my friend said confidently over the telephone. "He said I'll get chances at a lot of Pope and Young bucks." When our conversation ended, I hung up the phone worried that my friend might be a bit overconfident. And in November my fears were confirmed when he called to tell me that the hunt hadn't quite gone as planned.

Rut dates are a point of contention among many deer hunters. Charlie Alsheimer says the dates are variable, a belief he explains in Chapter 3.

Deer hunting's allure is its mystery. We deer hunters search for answers, but there is only so much science that can be applied. Deer, after all, are relatively intelligent animals and each whitetail is an individual with unique responses to different stimuli, forage and habitat preferences. That's why some old bucks become downright famous for their uncanny abilities to elude hunters.

The Veterans on Deer Myths & Facts

I thought it might be interesting to ask some veteran deer hunters out there about what we really know and don't know about whitetails. A lot of us have picked up theories espoused by other hunters and have kept hold of these ideas without any real basis. By the end of this section, maybe we'll destroy a couple of myths that had you confused, or confirm a couple of whitetail tendencies that you've noticed in the deer woods.

Charlie Alsheimer
Myth: "Breeding in the North always happens in mid- to late November."
Myth: "You can buy big antlers out of a bag."

Fact: You gotta have age. Without age you don't have big antlers, and it doesn't matter how much money you throw at it with food plots."

Greg Miller
Myth: "Big bucks always travel into the wind."
Fact: "In the north-woods where we have wolves, you watch these deer in the morning, and they're using their eyes and ears big time. With the wind at their tail when they're going to their bedding areas, it's my theory that they are trying to determine if something is following them. When they go to bed and to sleep, they're vulnerable. By putting the wind at their backs and using their nose, there's

In the same way that bedded bucks will put the wind at their backs, Greg Miller says he sees bucks that are wary of trailing predators tail-winding it as they head to bed.

absolutely no way that a wolf, man or whatever is following them into their sanctuary."

Myth: "The rubber boot thing."

Fact: "My friend's trailing hounds can follow him all over the woods, even when he's wearing his rubber boots. I wear whatever boots I want but treat them like the rest of my hunting clothes."

M. R. James

Myth: "One of the most persistent myths I hear involves spike bucks and the idea that all hunters should shoot spike bucks in order to rid the local whitetail gene pool of inferior animals."

Fact: "Whitetail authority Dr. James Kroll presents evidence of spikes growing into record-class bucks over the course of three to four seasons. While it might be true that spikes with inferior genetics living in nutrient-poor areas might never develop antlers that will draw a second look from most deer hunters, it's dead wrong to generalize and recommend that all spikes be shot to improve the quality of the herd."

North American Hunter *Bowhunting Advisory Council Member M. R. James points to the debate about spike buck potential as a persistent myth.*

Fact: "Most bucks taken by hunters are less than three years old. Why? Lots of serious deer hunters—myself included—are convinced that bucks get progressively smarter and harder to kill as they age. If it weren't for the annual rut when these big bucks lower their guard, or perhaps due to a liberal dose of blind luck, true trophy whitetails would rarely be taken. They're a different animal: reclusive, hunt-wise and totally unique compared to lesser bucks."

Gary Clancy

Myth: "Rattling might work in Texas, but it doesn't work where I hunt."

Fact: "I've rattled in bucks in 17 different states and provinces, and if I can do it, anyone can. The latitude and longitude a buck calls home has nothing to do with whether or not that buck will respond to rattling antlers. Herd composition, specifically the buck-to-doe ratio and the number of mature bucks within the herd, determine how effective rattling will be in any area. Hunting pressure, timing and weather are also major players."

Myth: "You can't fool a whitetail's nose, so there's no sense in wasting money on odor control."

Fact: "The technology is now available for us to be able to dramatically reduce our human odor. Products like scent-free soaps and detergents, odor-reducing sprays and powders

Rubber boots can help control foot scent, and Gary Clancy believes that odor control efforts can beat a whitetail's nose from time to time.

and carbon-activated suits—when used diligently and as part of a total odor control plan—really work. It's not easy, but it can be done."

Myth: "Hunting scrape lines is the most effective technique to use during the rut."

Fact: "Scrape lines provide a narrow window of opportunity. There is only about a week, 10 days max, when hunting over scrape lines should be your major focus. This 10-day period occurs just prior to the first wave of does entering estrous. Once that happens, forget scrapes."

Mark Kayser

Myth: "Calling works under any condition, even in hard-hunted areas. Success mostly depends on the mood of the buck at the particular time that he hears a call."

Myth: "Genetics is more important than age when it comes to producing large-racked deer."

Fact: "Rutting whitetails move, even in the face of moderate hunting pressure. Their desire to procreate outweighs the danger in some cases."

Fact: "Whitetails can tolerate a certain level of human activity without vacating their home range entirely. Suburban deer prove that point."

This buck didn't let a high sun keep him from going about his travels.

Does Midday Really Pay?

So far it hasn't paid off big for me, but I know enough hunters who have seen enough big bucks in the middle of the day to keep me hunting as many hours of the day as I possibly can.

In fact, I wonder if sometimes I might not be better served by starting my hunt later in the morning so that I can make it through the late morning and early afternoon hours on stand. There are times, even during the rut, when deer movement doesn't seem to be as good as it should be early and late in the day. In my experience, these times coincide with full moons and clear nights when I think deer do a lot of traveling and chasing after dark. These are supposed to be the times when midday pays. The thinking is that the deer bed before daylight, move about a little during midday and then might not move again until right at dark.

In a midwestern deer camp recently, a group of North American Hunting Club Bowhunting Advisory Council members endured some difficult hunting despite good hunting dates and decent weather. The full moon, though, might have been a factor and, indeed, the hunters who spent some time on stand right during the middle of the day saw some deer movement. It was not spectacular, mind you, but it was more deer movement than one could find at camp.

Outdoor writer Gary Clancy was in that neck of the woods during the same time as our hunt. I've had the good fortune of sharing deer camps with Clancy in the past and know that he is as dedicated as white-tailed deer hunters get. Clancy says that he's averaged 25 all-day sits each year during the past 15 years of his hunting career. That's a lot. Here are Clancy's thoughts on

whether or not all day pays.

"There are two times during the season when I feel that sitting on stand all day dramatically increases my odds of seeing deer," Clancy says. "One is the rut. When the rut is in progress, that buck of a lifetime could just as easily show up at high noon as at the more traditional hours of first and last light. The other factor is hunting pressure."

Clancy says that his rut hunt buck sightings are highest early in the morning, but that midday (from 11 a.m. to 2 p.m.) beats evening by nearly two to one. Hunting pressure, like that early in the firearms season, also keeps Clancy on stand all day. Since hunters are moving a lot during midday, that means they are causing deer to move about as well.

Look at it like this. A lot of deer are killed when the sun is high in the sky. You have to be out there hunting, for it to happen to you.

Hunters who have tried it have seen the results that midday hunting can offer during particular times of the season.

BEATING BUCK FEVER

I've only told a few people this story and have never written about it before. Sometimes I think it was just a dream. But it really happened.

A TALE OF BUCK FEVER

What 13-year-old deer hunters lack in ability, they make up for in optimism. So my school buddy, David, and I headed out to the woodlots while our fathers and the other adults in camp took a few hours off for lunch. It was a warm, sunny day in the middle of the nine-day Wisconsin gun deer season. Odds were not good that the two of us would lay eyes on a single deer, much less the giant buck that still haunts me.

A couple hours into our "hunt" we decided to head back to see what was going on at camp. Cresting a small hill in the muddy picked cornfield, I skidded to a stop. About 150

yards out was a group of four or five does and fawns on the edge of a narrow strip of still-standing corn. Evidently, they'd been pushed from an adjacent woodlot and were trying to decide which way to head for safety. David and I were slowly crouching down when I glanced to the opposite side of the standing corn. There, head low and swiftly sneaking in our direction, a fine buck had quickly determined his escape route; we two greenhorn hunters happened to be lying there, and he didn't know it.

One would think that two hunters each with five slugs loaded into shotguns less than 20 yards from a standing broadside buck would be unfair. And in our case it was incredibly unfair to us. Despite our firepower, that buck had every advantage. He had tall, wide, white antlers gleaming in the sunlight. He had those hypnotic black eyes that cast a spell on our young brains. David and I deserved to tag that buck and drag him back to camp to show off to our dads and the others. We had done everything right. We were out there hunting, we saw the buck before he saw us, and we waited patiently until he stopped just 20 yards out with nothing between us but air and opportunity. Then something weird happened.

David's gun went off just as I was aiming my gun and squeezing the trigger, and the blast sent my first shot somewhere well over the buck's head. He was in high gear by the time we shucked those pump guns and sent more lead in his general direction. And he kept on running. I'd bet that neither of us put a slug within 10 feet of that buck. I asked David what happened on his first shot, and he could barely speak; it seemed as though he didn't even remember.

We tracked that buck the best we could for probably half-a-mile. No hair, no blood, no nothing. So we went back to camp and told our story; and that's as far as it's gone until now.

UNDERSTANDING BUCK FEVER

Buck fever. We had it bad that day. I've felt tinges of it come back time to time in the years since, but I deal with the

You've done everything right to get to this point. Now it comes down to waiting for a good shot and mastering the mental aspect of hunting.

The sight of a big white-tailed buck can be mesmerizing.

symptoms a lot better these days. Who knows what'll happen, though, if I ever see an honest-to-goodness Boone and Crockett Club buck up close? All we deer hunters can do to beat buck fever is to learn to understand it. So let's try to find a cure.

North American Hunter "Media Watch" columnist James Swan is a former psychologist who was in private practice for 10 years helping athletes and entertainers deal with the stresses of performance situations. Swan has a degree in environmental psychology from the University of Michigan and has taught psychology at the University of Michigan, University of Oregon, and University of Washington. Of equal importance is his vast experience as an avid deer hunter who has pursued whitetails with both firearm and bow. Here's how he defines buck fever.

"Stage fright, buck fever and target panic all fall under the notion of performance anxiety, where you have to contain excitement and focus on your concentration, in order to maintain a level of concentration and relaxation and attention to execute," Swan says. "While practice helps, it's no substitute for the real thing.

Experience is something that helps many deer hunters overcome buck fever. The more deer you harvest, the less you will be controlled by buck fever.

"When we talk about hunting, there are many skills that get you to this point. Shooting at a target is one thing, but the excitement, I believe, is heightened in hunting because you can't control the animal. So as soon as you see or hear that animal, it adds the element of 'What is he going to do?' And the additional concern that you're going to kill it. You tend to be more empathetic with something that's closer to you. So people feel more empathy toward a mammal than a bird and more toward a bird than a fish."

LOOKING FOR CURES

Swan says that some crossover cures apply to all types of performance anxiety (buck fever).

"What you work with for people dealing with performance anxiety are two things," Swan says. "One of which is that it's associated in part with fear of failure. When I used to work with athletes I would have them imagine what they were doing and freeze-frame on who's watching you. That person is often your most serious critic. Then you replace that person with a new watcher. Have Fred Bear standing there with you if you like, if you want someone there coaching you. Ultimately, as you practice more, that splits away and then you move into a zone where you can concentrate, relax, focus and shut off everything else so that it becomes easy."

Swan related how Tom Hanks, upon winning his Oscar, thanked his high school acting coach and said how he imagined his coach sitting there next to him on his stool while he was acting. Concentrating specifically on buck fever, though, Swan has five suggestions that might help you better deal with the excitement and anxiety.

One: "A lot of people in sports performance use an affirmation like, 'I will hit the bull's eye' or 'I will make this shot.' With hunting, the phrase a lot of people use is, 'If I shoot, let me kill clean or miss clean,' and that helps you focus."

Two: "Try a simple breathing exercise basketball players shooting free throws use: If you're really excited, and your bow or gun is shaking, breathe in slowly while counting to yourself 1, 2, 3; then hold 1, 2, 3; then exhale 1, 2, 3. Repeat. That's used for treating people with all kinds of anxiety situations."

Three: "To improve concentration, pick that spot to shoot at. Learn to visualize the arrow or bullet going there before you shoot it. Golfers will tell you that their game is 90 percent between the ears. Visualize every shot before it happens."

Four: "Practice distance recognition to remove guesswork. If you're worrying 'Which pin should I use?' that's additional anxiety piled on top of everything else. Remove extraneous things like that. If you're a bowhunter, shoot a lot and pace off distances so that you can judge those distances and know them by heart, so that it's an automatic process. Repetition is valuable, but the most important aspect is to practice with awareness so that there's improvement." Sounds like a good argument for a laser rangefinder doesn't it?

Five: "The last thing is really a kind of checklist that you need to develop ahead of time to reduce more extraneous

Don't look him in the eye, control your breathing and think positively.

things that would interfere. Physical conditioning: Are you in good shape? Can you retrieve the animal? What will you do with the animal? All those things that sort of hang there in the subconscious. Have all of those things thought out, done and out of the way."

Most of all, Swan says, expect that you're going to be excited. All deer hunters, even the most veteran among us, get excited when we spot a whitetail and position for a shot.

"Be patient with yourself," Swan says. "It's going to be exciting. Your heart is going to go thumping. Go along with it and let it happen. That's one of the things that happens to people; we get afraid of the excitement. Allow yourself to be excited and feel good about it. That knocks the level of anxiety down one notch right there."

And it makes deer hunting all the more fun and helps us toward our goal of hunting whitetails successfully.

A rangefinder can help you eliminate one of the unknowns that often result in flashes of buck fever.

BLOOD-TRAILING BASICS

I wish I could say that all the blood trails I've been on have been short and that I've found a dead deer at the end of every one. Neither is the case.

I have been on a lot of blood trails. But just about when I think I've seen it all, I encounter circumstances or conditions I've never faced and find myself becoming an even better blood-trailer because of it.

There is no sure-fire blood-trailing approach that works under every condition. Every blood trail is a little different. And each one requires a different strategy. Knowing what to do and when to do it can only be learned by blood-trailing. I can give you some ideas here. But, like so many other things about deer hunting, the most important piece of advice is this: Put in your time. Help your family and friends whenever you get the opportunity to spend time helping track a wounded deer. There is no better teacher than experience.

All that said, we come to this: when to track, when to wait, and when to pull off a track entirely. These are the points of contention in many a deer hunting discussion. But no matter how loudly your buddies argue about the right way and wrong way to track a wounded deer, until you're there and see what's before you, it's difficult to judge somebody else's decision.

READING THE HIT

For gun hunters, it's often more difficult to tell exactly

A lot of hair and little blood at the sight of the hit is usually a bad sign. Often, though, it can mean that the deer is not wounded at all.

where a bullet made impact than for a bowhunter to tell where his arrow hit. Recoil often blurs the view of the animal. If you're hunting with a friend or guide, he'll probably have a much better idea of where the bullet hit. And this information is vital in determining your blood-trailing strategy in case the deer doesn't drop within view.

Bowhunters are well served to use brightly colored fletching on their arrows for this very reason. I like white and fluorescent 5-inch fletches on my arrows because it's easier for me to track the arrow's flight and note the point of impact than if I'm using dark-colored fletching. Don't worry: I've never had a deer spook because it saw my bright fletching. I've seen bowhunters use camo fabric over the fletches of the arrows in their quiver, but I really don't think it's necessary. Cover them if you like, but by all means use the bright fletches. You'll be amazed at the difference.

READING THE DEER

Some hunters look for a deer to tuck its tail tightly as sign of a good hit. Others think that if it kicks up its back legs it means that the deer was hit in a particular spot. To me, these tendencies are not entirely reliable.

I've seen lung-shot deer raise their tails, run 75 yards, then tip over and die. I've seen deer hit in the front leg kick up their hind legs and I've seen deer shot in the paunch do the same thing. This is why reading the hit is so crucial.

And while the initial behavior of the deer at the moment of impact might not be a reliable indicator of what kind of tracking job you might encounter, I do concentrate hard on what the deer does after it's hit and before it disappears from view.

If the shot felt good and the deer hunches slightly and runs hard all the way until disappearing, I take that as a good sign that the deer is well hit. Though I've heard stories from other bowhunters about deer that were lung-shot or heart-shot jumping a short distance, stopping and acting like nothing was wrong before falling over, I've never seen it myself. Doesn't mean that it can't happen. But the deer that I've

Closely mark the deer's travel route and note its body language after the hit. This information is crucial to making decisions on the blood trail.

seen run a short distance, stop and look back, are usually not hit in the vital chest cavity.

Of course, if you're fortunate enough to get a good look at blood on the side of a fleeing deer, you're way ahead of the game. In fact, you might have time to find the deer again in your scope or binoculars for a closer view of the wound. And while this is helpful, it's even more important to note the deer's exact route and location when it was hit and when it disappeared from view. In fact, marking the deer's entire route of travel from point of impact to disappearance will help dramatically when you come back to begin the tracking job.

FIRST BLOOD

I always start at the location where the deer was standing at the time of the shot. This might be moments after the shot

A wide area of splattered, bright blood where the deer was standing at the shot means greater odds of a short blood trail.

or hours, depending on whether I'm bow or gun hunting and what kind of hit I think I have. Don't run out to where the deer disappeared and start there. You'll have missed important clues that can help you later on in the process. Start at the beginning.

Of course, you're looking for blood, hair and, if you're bowhunting, your arrow. A lot of foamy pink blood right at the start means that you can get on the blood trail and bank on the deer being less than 100 yards away. A lot of hair and little or no blood at the start means that you might have a problem. Again, as I said earlier, there is no blanket statement that can be made about how far a deer will go with a particular hit. So be deliberate and gather as much information on the ground as you can.

An average deer has approximately 8 units of blood, or 6,400 cubic centimeters. To go into shock because of blood loss, the deer has to lose about half of its blood. According to *North American Hunter* "Whitetails" columnist Larry Weishuhn, a whitetail can lose half of its blood and still survive if it has access to water, good nutrition and was in good physical condition at the time the wound occurred.

"That's why when an animal is wounded and loses any amount of blood it tends to head to water," Weishuhn says, "to replenish its body fluids and to cool off."

MARK THE TRAIL

Mark the trail as you go, especially if it's sketchy. And, if you have helpers, move together at the same pace with one person staying on the last blood at all times. Only when another person finds the next blood do you move on, and only after marking the last spot with flagging or other material that can be easily seen and retrieved later.

Too many trackers, if not working in concert, can mess up a trail. More people isn't always better when it comes to tracking a deer. At least not early in the process.

DECISIONS, DECISIONS

Suppose you know you have a deer that is not hit in the chest cavity. My general rule is to wait a minimum of four hours, in most of these cases, before tracking. With clear weather and cool temperatures, my odds of recovering the deer, I've learned, improve with this approach and I've never had a deer spoil in this amount of time. From there, I stay on the blood trail as long as I can readily follow it. That's especially true if I know that rain or snow is on the way and might obliterate the blood.

If I bump the deer and realize that it's still alive, it's decision time again. Some hunters choose to keep pushing the deer, especially if there's still blood on the ground. Others opt to pull off

This blood trail will be short. Despite a perfectly placed bullet, though, even deer shot with firearms sometimes travel more than 100 yards.

If during the course of your tracking you encounter the deer still alive, you have a decision to make. If you have a shot you can try to finish the deer. If not, you have to determine whether to pull off the track and let the deer bed, or keep pushing the deer.

the track, wait another couple hours and come back. There is no definitive answer to the tough question of whether to pursue or wait. But here's a guideline. If you have access to the country before you and can push the deer, I'd keep on it. Sometimes keeping a wounded deer moving and on its feet is the quickest way to recover it. If, however, you run the risk of pushing the deer onto posted property and know you might

Marking the trail as you go is critical. It's easy to lose last blood otherwise and can result in lost time trying to relocate the trail.

run into trouble as a result, you might be best advised to back off for another few hours in hopes that the deer will bed down.

USE GRIDS

Even if you run out of blood, there's hope. The deer might well be down only a short distance from last blood. In this particular scenario, the more help the better. Set up a grid pattern for you and your buddies to walk, in order to conduct a ground search of at least a quarter-mile square area at the end of the trail. This requires patience, diligence and powers of observation to pick out any part of a deer in the surround-

If you have extra help, it's wise for one or more hunters to flank the blood trail and watch ahead in an attempt to spot the deer.

Lantern light floods a wide area of the ground and works well for picking up droplets of blood

Blood-trailing is difficult, tedious work. But it is also extremely rewarding when all that work pays off and you recover the deer. "Don't give up" are the three watch words.

ing cover. Maybe only the tip of an antler tine or a few white belly hairs will be visible.

One thing's for certain. If you're like me, you remember the long blood trails and the anguish of a misplaced shot a lot more readily than the perfect shots and the short blood trails. That's a good thing. Because it makes us better trackers and helps us do an even better job of recovering these magnificent animals and putting excellent venison on our tables. Never give up on a blood trail. We owe every ounce of our effort to recovering the game we shoot. Put in your time at the practice range, be disciplined in your shot selection, and then, as an outdoor writer friend of mine used to say, "Aim hard."

SCENT-FREE: THE IMPOSSIBLE DREAM?

"That's all marketing. I don't care what you wear or spray on to try to beat a deer's nose, you can't do it. If a deer gets downwind, nothing you do is going to matter."

I've heard those words more times than I can count and from a lot of hunters whom I respect. Still, the skepticism hasn't caused me to change my approach to trying to beat a deer's nose. Here's my reasoning; maybe it's flawed, but you be the judge and you decide whether or not trying to control your own human scent is worth it.

DEALING WITH THE SKEPTICS

If the skeptics are right that none of the products currently on the market can contain human scent well enough to

beat a whitetail's nose, that means that the guy who smokes, doesn't shower before hunting or wash his hunting clothes regularly, wears his hunting clothing inside the house exposing them to all kinds of odors and then wrestles with Rover before hopping in his pickup, is just as well off as the guy who goes to great lengths to be as scent-free as possible.

Now don't object, Mr. Skeptic. That is what you are arguing. If you say that a downwind deer is going to smell you no matter what, you are saying that smoking on stand or wearing the same hunting clothes for a week without washing is okay. We all know, after all, that an upwind deer isn't going to smell us despite that incredible nose. Nor is a crosswind deer. Right? It's only when that deer gets the wind or thermals from us to him that we're in danger. So again, if we can't contain human scent, then it's a free-for-all out there.

I'm sorry to sound sarcastic, but that's the skeptic's argument. "You gotta hunt with the wind," they say chest out and full of pride for their incredible assessment of white-tailed deer hunting. To that I say, "Duh." That's Deer Hunting 101. Tell me something I didn't know. Tell me something my dad didn't tell me the very first day I went deer hunting.

Playing the wind is a given. But, ah, the beauty and mystery and magic of deer hunting is that I've never figured out a way to ensure that the deer are going to appear upwind of my stand site. Maybe the skeptics never have a deer show up downwind. Maybe they are so perfect in their stand

Scent control efforts and playing the wind go hand-in-hand. Getting consistently close to whitetails requires a serious concerted effort to beat their sense of smell.

selection that the deer come out perfectly upwind just as predicted. Or maybe the downwind deer simply smelled the skeptic way before the skeptic ever had a clue that there was a deer approaching from that direction.

Scent Control Matters

That's my bet. I don't claim to be the best deer hunter around, but I've spent enough time in the deer woods to say with complete confidence that scent control does matter.

And despite the skeptics reading this who are jumping up and down or slamming the book shut, you can improve your odds on downwind deer by understanding the various methods for controlling human scent. Marketing aside, I've seen it. It's happened to me on more than one occasion that deer have approached extremely close from perfectly downwind. The skeptics can argue that the wind was carrying my scent over the deer's head or whatever, but I hunted for a lot of years without the benefit of some of the products on the market today. And in those days, I got busted by whitetails A LOT more than I do today.

Yes, some deer still smell me. However, many others have taken an arrow or bullet at a downwind position before they

ever knew I was there. If the skeptics are right, that never happens. But it does. And they're wrong. Read on to discover why.

Play the Wind Right

I agree wholeheartedly with the skeptics who say that you can't rely on products or other scent-killing methods to help you defy the wind when it comes to whitetail hunting. That is not what I attempt to do. I place my stands first considering the prevailing wind. If it's a stand that I might only hunt for a day or two, I rely more on the local weather forecast. Prevailing wind doesn't mean anything if you're on a short timeframe. It might blow south for five days, so who cares if northwest is the prevailing wind direction?

After I've assessed the wind, thermals and topography, and selected my stand site, I take it a step further by doing everything in my power to control human scent. In a nutshell, this means showering regularly before hunts with scent-free soap and shampoo. Washing my hunting clothing regularly with scent-free laundry detergent. Wearing a scent-control suit with activated carbon. Spraying my hunting outerwear with human scent-destroyer sprays. Wearing knee-high rubber boots to contain foot-scent on the way to my stand. Then

Deer are not always searching for the smell of a predator. During the rut, when they are distracted, a small amount of human scent might go unnoticed.

storing my hunting clothing in air-tight containers away from household and other foreign odors.

I guarantee you that all this makes a difference. Think about this. You're in your treestand during the chase phase of the rut, does are not quite in heat and bucks are on the move, searching helter-skelter for receptive does. You can gawk at deer trails as long as you want, but there's no way that you can predict exactly where that deer is going to show. And if you're a bowhunter who has to wait for a good shooting angle and a clear lane to that buck's vitals, it might mean that the buck has to cross downwind before that shot opportunity presents itself. So tell me, if this is the biggest buck you've ever seen in your life, are you going to take the skeptic's view that it doesn't matter? Are you going to resign yourself to the fact that the buck is going to smell you anyway and you might as well hang your bow back on the hook or lay your firearm back across your lap? Or, is it worth the

Nothing will turn a whitetail inside out like a snout full of human scent. But scent control measures can let deer come within range before they smell a rat.

chance that you eliminate and contain enough human scent that the buck doesn't catch you until it's too late?

Or what about this? Under any hunting condition there is a maximum distance at which a whitetail can smell us. Now, does that maximum distance decrease if I take some of the scent-controlling precautions that I've already outlined? Let me put it another way. Can a whitetail smell certain odors farther away than others? If so, and that maximum distance is variable, I'll make the argument that the rifle hunter is also well served to take scent control to the Nth degree. Maybe that buck won't smell you until he's already in your sights. But if you haven't taken care about controlling human scent, maybe he'll smell you before you ever lay eyes on him.

CONTROL SCENT AS BEST YOU CAN

If you are sloppy about scent control, you're dead on downwind deer. I'm convinced of this. Gun or bow. However, if you'll take the precautions that I'll outline later, you will get opportunities that you never would have imagined. I've seen bucks that were distracted by the rut or other deer in the area, and I'm convinced that some individual deer under these conditions are not at all times trying to identify danger with their noses. Now, if that is indeed the case, a couple of human scent molecules might go unnoticed. If, however, you allowed Rover to rub up against you and drool on your glove, or if your clothing still reeks of cigarette smoke from the butts you had in the truck on the way out, it's quite likely that you'll get that deer's attention.

You can bet that every deer is going to smell you under those conditions—distracted deer or not. On the other end of the spectrum, a tuned-up doe that's heard or seen something she didn't like to begin with and then marches downwind into your scent stream is probably going to bust you, even if you've done everything perfectly with regard to controlling human scent. I'll agree, you cannot do a 100 percent perfect job.

Get my drift? Or what about this one? You're hunting the one stand option available to you at a particular time. Yes, I preach the merits of having multiple stand sites available at all times and staying mobile, but that's the ideal world. In the real world, on outfitted hunts, for example, that stand you're dropped at is your stand for that half-day or whole-day hunt. You climb up, yep, everything's right, trail there, wind here, then the breeze switches.

Okay, I hear the skeptic saying crawl down and get out of there because it's better to waste that half day or whole day than to mess up the deer. I can buy that argument if you have a ton of time to hunt those particular deer. But what if it's your vacation? Or what if you've saved a long time for this particular outfitted deer hunt? Wind switches, so you bag it? Not me in that situation.

Last September I was hunting whitetails in Montana. (See "September Western Success" in Chapter 2.) The outfitter had done an excellent job of finding a morning stand far enough from a feeding area so that we could sneak in without the deer in the fields seeing us.

During the five-day hunt we saw bucks every day from that stand despite the fact that the wind blew from a couple of different directions. We never got the north wind we wanted. The last day of the hunt, a bunch of deer passed on a downwind trail, caught a whiff of our human scent and hurried past toward their bedding area. It was a foggy day, the worst kind if you're a deer hunter worried about deer smelling you. Still, the deer didn't spook badly. In fact, the last deer in line, the biggest buck we'd seen during our five-day hunt watched the other deer move off without their tails raised. So he continued along a different trail he'd chosen to bed that morning. It took him to within 15 yards of my tree and out onto an upwind sage flat. I shot him at 40 yards, and that was that. The other deer never blew to alert him, and I filled my tag with my best bow-killed buck ever.

Best of all, I didn't feel that I had to give up on a great morning stand location. In fact, it really was the only good morning stand available to us. Like I said, if you have the luxury to play the wind to your advantage and leave a stand when the wind blows wrong, do it. But my feeling is that most of us don't have that luxury.

SCENT CONTROL METHODS

Okay, if you're with me so far, you're probably asking how it's done. Let's start before we even get dressed for the hunt.

Personal Odors

Cleanliness, when it comes to deer hunting, is next to godliness. Since whitetail hunts are not remote backpack hunts, you have the opportunity to shower regularly using scent-free soaps and shampoos. These products are readily available at sporting goods stores. Some of the manufacturers are Robinson Labs, Wildlife Research Center and Atsko Inc.

Breath is another consideration. During a hunt you're exhaling 250 volume liters of air every hour. It does you no good to take a shower with scent-free soap and then eat a veggie omelet packed with bell peppers and onions. Brush your teeth before hunting and then eat an apple. Chlorophyll tablets from a drug store can also eliminate breath odor. Well-known outdoor communicator and deer hunter Gary Clancy gargles with NO-ODOR liquid from Atsko Inc. NO-ODOR can also be sprayed onto clothing to kill odor-causing the bacteria.

It is estimated that a whitetail's nose is 25 times more acute than that of a human. You can either surrender or try to do something about it.

Underlayer Clothing

From there, let's consider the clothing you'll wear under a scent-adsorbing suit. Underwear, socks, pants and shirts should all be washed regularly in scent-free, UV brightener-free detergent and then stored in an air-tight container between hunts. For additional protection, after dressing you can spray down this underlayer with scent-destroying sprays like Scent Shield.

Scent-Adsorbing Suit

Then comes that scent-adsorbing suit. A couple of examples are the Scent-Lok suit by ALS Enterprises and the ScentBlocker suit by Robinson Labs. Both utilize activated carbon that helps capture and hold human scent caused by bacteria. These suits can be machine washed every couple of weeks or so during heavy use. Again, they should be washed in a scent-free detergent, and there is a detergent on the market from Robinson Labs intended specifically for these garments.

From there, drying the suit in your clothes dryer for 15 minutes or so on high heat recharges the activated carbon. The suit should be kept in an air-tight container, preferably in your hunting vehicle, and put on only after you arrive at your parking spot. This will help you avoid contaminating it with household and other scents. Most of these suits also come with a cap, facemask or headcover of some kind. Wear it. A lot of human scent is held in your hair, and the headcovers are designed to also capture some of your breath.

Head-to-toe activated charcoal or carbon suits, along with scent-destroying sprays and breath control, all improve your odds.

Deer camp is a smelly place. Keep your hunting clothes in an airtight container to avoid contaminating them with foreign odors.

Outerwear

Finally, consider your outerwear. Some of the newer scent-adsorbing suits are built with soft, quiet material that can be worn as your outermost garment. If, however, you wear something over the top, this must also be stored in an air-tight container and put on after you arrive afield. Then spray yourself down as completely as possible with a scent-destroying spray like those already mentioned.

Rubber Boots

Knee-high rubber boots are the final element to help you avoid leaving human foot-scent on the way to your stand. For cold-weather hunting, some boot manufacturers now offer knee-high rubber boots with up to 1,000 grams of Thinsulate insulation. If it's really cold, a heavy pac boot is fine so long as it has a rubber bottom. I still spray my rubber boots down with scent-destroying sprays. If you haven't already figured it out, I'm paranoid when it comes to human scent.

Summing Up Scent Control

If you follow this method and are diligent about controlling human scent, I'll guarantee that you'll notice the results. Nothing can make up for sloppy hunting. You must pay attention to the wind when choosing stand sites. But I've been deer hunting long enough to know that the deer woods is a dynamic place that is changing all the time. And things don't always go as planned. I know I'm up against the most finely tuned nose of any big game animal in North America. You can surrender or try to do something about it.

Chapter 2

DEER HUNTING BY THE SEASON

No two deer hunting days are exactly alike. Maybe that's the allure of the whitetail woods. Unpredictability means anticipation. Anticipation means excitement. Excitement means adrenaline. For us whitetail hunters, there is no greater high than that pulsing through our veins each new day as we head afield.

In this chapter we will take you through a year in the life of the whitetail hunter, minus the rut. That subject is reserved for a chapter unto itself a bit further on. Here we're going to talk scouting and explain what you can learn about deer year-round that will help you come hunting season. But we'll do it in a "real-world" kind of way that understands the fact that you have more to do in the off-season than scout full-time for deer.

From there, we'll go hunting. We'll head out right from the opening bell in August or September with bows in hand. With a gun tag in our pockets a couple of months later, we'll see what firearms season brings and look for ways to succeed despite the increased hunting pressure.

But we won't stop there. With a late-season muzzleloader license or empty bow tag to fill, we'll stay on the whitetail trail after the rut and the general firearms season is gone. It'll be a tough hunt to be sure, but before you know it, deer season will be gone. And you'll be dreaming about next year all over again.

Come along to the dynamic deer woods where we'll try to keep one step ahead of this incredible animal.

REAL-WORLD SCOUTING

Some time ago I received a letter from my friend Charles J. Alsheimer of Bath, New York. You've probably heard Charlie's name before, since he is an exceptional source of white-tailed deer hunting knowledge. His photography is incredible, and his hundreds of magazine articles have helped thousands of deer hunters better understand the deer woods.

Charlie's letter to me that day outlined a few ideas for stories that we might publish in *North American Hunter* magazine. One especially caught my eye. It was titled, "Can You Really Pattern Deer?" It didn't take much thought on my part to decide that this one deserved an assignment letter. And, once again, Charlie did not disappoint with the message of his article.

I hunted with Charlie once in northeastern Wisconsin during the first few weeks of the bowhunting season. We were both in unfamiliar territory as guests at a hunting camp. After the first day of the hunt, most of us hunters were complaining about the lack of deer sightings and wondered why things

were so slow. Charlie had an answer. He'd crawled out of his treestand midmorning and started poking around, following deer trails here and there until he got near the property line and found the answer. Just across the fence was a deer stand with a bait pile (legal in Wisconsin) nearby. The neighbors, it turns out, were baiting the place pretty heavily and had the best whitetail food source going at that particular time. Needless to say, the rest of the five-day hunt was slow. Nobody in our camp killed a deer.

It wasn't the landowner's fault. He'd done a fine job setting the stands on his place. He lived in a cabin on the property, was retired and had more time than the average deer hunter to keep tabs on the whitetails. But he'd been thrown a curve. It could have been thrown by Mother Nature with a sudden acorn drop or harvest of an adjacent crop field. Or a doe could come into heat and throw the local bucks into an unpatternable frenzy. All of these "unknowns" and more formed the backbone of Charlie's article that I referred to earlier.

With so many things changing so rapidly in the deer woods from September through December, how can we ever hope to stay on top of it while working a full-time job, getting our kids to ball practice, keeping the dogs exercised and doing chores around the house? And if everything's going to change from opening day to closing anyway, what good is all this scouting and patterning stuff that so many deer hunting writers preach over and over again?

Charlie's point was clear when I read his letter. Most deer hunters can't dedicate the time to scouting and patterning as it's described in most deer hunting articles. So where does that leave us? How does the real-world deer hunter increase his odds of intercepting deer come fall? What is the critical information that he or she must be able to gather from "scouting?"

LAND-HO!

You have to have a place to hunt to have a place to scout. There's a revelation, right? Land access is a

A plat book and detailed map of an area can provide vital information that can help you find a good deer hunting spot.

more difficult challenge every season, it seems, as land is leased or purchased by hunters who have a lot more money than I do. Maybe you've felt the pinch too.

But I'll bet that there are places right in the same county where you live that offer deer hunting opportu-

Once you have permission to hunt a piece of property or have located a public area, a topo map will shed light on potential deer travel routes.

nity if you know where to find them and who to talk to. Combine a good road map with a county plat map (available at most banks or county offices) and you can quickly determine who owns what.

My brother-in-law, Mike, and I rely heavily on a plat map when we pheasant hunt in Iowa. We generally head down to hunt without any land access open to us and simply knock on doors once we find some good habitat and match it up with the owner listed in the plat book. Who knows, you might see in the plat book that a friend of a friend or a distant relative owns a choice little chunk of ground that you didn't know about! Or you might notice a little 40- or 80-acre parcel of county or state property open to hunting. You might be surprised how little hunting pressure some of these out-of-the-way public lands see.

SCOUTING DEFINED

First off, scouting is a term that I think most deer hunters assume means searching for deer sign before the season begins. But if you're a bowhunter and the season opens in September, August scouting might only give you a fine case of poison ivy or require a blood transfusion to replace ounces lost to the mosquitos. The August woods in many places are not fit to be scouted. Foliage is too thick to see much of anything. Deer trails are mostly invisible, rubs have not yet appeared, most mast crops aren't available yet to deer ... it's just

A great day of hunting yields a big gobbler and some dandy sheds that provide clues to deer movements in the area.

plain tough to come away with anything that will give you any information to hang your hat on.

That said, there are some fine times out of season to scout for whitetails.

SPRING SCOUTING

A lot of the places where I hunt whitetails in the Upper Midwest are the same places where I chase wild turkeys in the spring. Since turkey hunting often requires you to cover a lot of country each day, you can learn a lot about the lay of the land where you might be deer hunting come fall. And, in

Turkeys don't leave trails like this! Since a lot of deer hunters pursue wild turkeys over the same ground where they whitetail hunt later on, spring is a fine time to gather information on what the deer are doing. As the countryside changes, so do deer patterns.

Late summer field watching is still important to get a read on where deer are feeding and which individual bucks are using the area.

my estimation at least, learning the land is what scouting is all about.

Say you cross a well-worn deer trail while out turkey hunting in spring and plan to set up on that trail come fall. That might be enough information to help you kill a deer, but a properly scouted piece of deer hunting country should tell you a lot more. I figure I've got a place scouted when I can walk out on that piece of property and tell you where everything is. The topography, the tree types, the trails, the feed, the brush, the fields, everything. That's your goal in scouting. If you scout with your nose to the ground looking for trails and tracks and droppings, you'll miss entirely too much of what is around you—and that might be a lot more important in the long run than seeing another deer track a few feet in front of your nose.

I know, I know. If you're focused on killing that old gobbler, you don't have time to scout for deer hunting stands at the same time. That's true. But a good turkey hunter scouts a piece of property before turkey season. And every step you take in the country where you'll deer hunt come fall is valuable to you later; even if you're after turkeys, rabbits, mush-

rooms, squirrels or some simple relaxation with the family. And spring is a great time to be out in the woods.

Another great thing about spring scouting is that some important sign from the year before might still be visible. Scrapes, rubs and trails are all still there, just like they were last fall. And when you're hustling through the woods trying to intercept a loud-mouthed gobbler, you'll probably bump into whitetails along the way. And as you watch them hightail it over the ridge, you might take a second to make a mental note about whether the deer were feeding or bedded—and that's another single piece of an infinite puzzle.

SCOUT OUT TREES TOO

Another thing I'm always looking for whenever I'm in the deer woods is a tree where I can hang a stand. Whenever I come to a place that has good deer sign, my first look is usually up about 20 feet off the ground for a place where a treestand will blend into the surrounding cover and give me a good opportunity to kill a deer. I'll hunt from the ground if I have to, or if there's a made-to-order natural setup, but I'm

It's a tiny piece of sign but another step toward solving the puzzle.

always scouting for good trees.

And I'll tell you where this really pays off. Once the rut rolls around, a lot of the scouting I've done in spring, right before the season, and during the pre-rut gets thrown out the window. Not all of it, but some. Food sources are of less importance. Trails, scrapes and rubs are of less importance. During the rut, I need places where deer are going to travel.

Those spring turkey hunts or mushroom hunts might be the only real chance you have to check out the deer hunting country until right before season. In the real world there are summer vacations and all kinds of things to think about instead of deer. But come September, and that first velvet buck that you see in the alfalfa field at dusk, you'll start thinking about where to hang a stand again.

EARLY SEASON: FOOD SOURCES ARE KEY

Most early-season hunting takes place around food sources that are relatively visible. That means that if you're fortunate enough to live near where you deer hunt, you can keep tabs on the deer with a good set of binoculars or spotting scope in the evening.

I'll be honest. You can watch deer and study things all summer, but the days right before the season are the most important. Food sources are in a constant state of change. Alfalfa fields are being harvested three, four or five times, apples are ripening and dropping at different times from different trees. A day can make a huge difference. So if you're trying to scout for an early-season deer, you better put in some time right before the opener. Which trail a particular deer uses to enter a field, which direction he typically feeds once he gets out into the field and what time he gets to that field are all important considerations that must be weighed.

Week-old information for early-season deer is almost useless. Therefore, like I say, don't think that hunting whitetails successfully requires you to be conducting surveillance on the deer all summer long. Take the summer vacations. Go to all of your children's ballgames. Go fishing. And catch up on the chores around the house. Because come opening day, real-world scouting kicks into high gear.

IN-SEASON SCOUTING

Hopefully you know the lay of the land by now. Maybe you've pounded around out here for years; maybe you spent a week after a tom turkey. And maybe your early-season,

opening-day apple tree or agricultural field didn't pan out. Now what?

To me, scouting during the season is what separates successful deer hunters from unsuccessful ones. Here's where you have to be able to think on your feet and read the sign that you encounter. When the bachelor groups of bucks break up and the food sources change, it might appear that all those whitetails have vanished. They haven't, of course, but you need to go after them.

I have a rule when it comes to deer stands. It's a three-strike rule. If I hunt a stand for a morning, afternoon and then again a second day, and don't see a deer within bow range, I move my stand. And sometimes a stand doesn't even get three strikes. If the weather and wind are perfect for two sits, and it doesn't pan out, I'm moving.

This way, I get to cover more of the country and increase the odds that I'm going to bump into whitetails along the way. A lot of times a stand doesn't pan out, but I see whitetail movement at a distance. Hunting and scouting are really synonymous in a lot of cases. You're looking. Way too many deer hunters sit on a stand where they killed a big buck years ago. And they sit there, and they sit there, and they sit there.

Having a feel for what type of cover the local whitetails use for bedding will help you determine stand locations for intercepting them on their way in and out.

Food, food, food. Don't forget the food.

And maybe they see some deer.

You'll be surprised what you might learn if you'll be flexible and move and continue to scout during the season. You might find a well-worn trail carved deep into the soil along a wide-open grassy fenceline. Maybe it's even within view of the road or some houses and you figure that there isn't a whitetail in its right mind that would travel this trail in daylight. Most hunters I know would keep walking, looking for a more "conventional" location for a stand. A few hunters I know will put a stand anywhere they think they have a chance to kill a deer. And those guys are the successful ones. Maybe that fenceline has only one tree fit for a stand, or maybe you have to hunt from the ground or dig a pit blind, if legal. I know this much: If you're not hunting fresh deer sign, you're not scouting, no matter how good the spot might look for other reasons. Great funnels or travel corridors are only great when deer are using them.

The true test for any deer hunting location is hunting it. Scouting provides information, but only hunting produces the results.

Even though you think you might be hunting the perfect travel corridor, you have to keep tabs on whether or not the sign in your area is fresh.

OPENING DAY

I know hunters who scoff at the idea of bowhunting for whitetails early in the season, when layers of thick green choke the deer woods and mosquitoes drone on patrol in the summer-like air. "It's not worth it until the rut gets going," an old-timer used to tell me. "Deer aren't moving now. Too hot. Might see some does and fawns, but I'm saving my tag for that big buck that'll be around during the rut."

For a long time I figured that man was right about early-season whitetails. But since I started spending more time in a treestand early in the season, I'm convinced that those weeks in September and October are just as good as the rut. In some cases, the early hunting might even be better.

I know what you're thinking. The blood loss from all those early-season mosquito bites has made me lightheaded. Maybe. But there are two Pope and Young white-tailed bucks at the taxidermist as I write this. I took one on August 31, and the other on September 14. Though I hunted some prime whitetail country in late October and all of November, when the rut should have been smoking, all I have to show for those long days in a treestand are empty tags. In fact, I saw more quality bucks during my pre-rut hunts than I did during the rut.

Granted, maybe it was just coincidence. Right place, right time. Wrong place, wrong time. Maybe hunting pressure, weather or other factors influenced deer movement. You know what, though, I killed a third buck in January in Louisiana ... well after the rut was gone in that region. And the successful hunts all have one thing in common. The deer herd was in a more predictable movement pattern that revolved around feed.

PATTERNING

In the previous chapter I aggressively challenged the notion that any of us can nail down a mature buck's routine well enough to consistently intercept these deer. Few of us have the time it takes to locate a buck on a day-to-day

An advantage of early-season bowhunting: Bucks are traveling in bachelor groups. If you see one buck, you sometimes see them all for that spot.

basis. But I say this mostly from the perspective of a midwestern/eastern deer hunter used to trying to find whitetails in woodlots or forests. Spying a buck with any regularity under these conditions is almost impossible unless you have a home near a preferred feeding area.

A friend of mine owns 80 acres in east-central Wisconsin and has a spotting scope set up by a window in his porch. From this vantage point, he can watch two agricultural fields that whitetails frequent. There's no doubt that he gets a look at each of the different deer on his place. Yet he might spot a good buck one evening and then not see him again for days at a time. Not much of a pattern.

Western whitetails are much more visible and, thus, more patternable as I learned during hunts in Idaho and Montana last fall (see page 50). Since a good share of the dense cover west of the Mississippi is more linear and includes riverbottoms and fencelines, travel routes are also easier to pin down. That doesn't mean that Western bucks come easy for the early-season hunter, but it is an advantage.

The bottom line is this: Whenever we deer hunters select a stand site, it is based on the thinking that deer will travel within range of that location. During the rut there is no pattern to follow at all. But there *are* funnels and bottlenecks and rub lines to hang your hat on. You can also sit near food sources in hopes that the does will bring the bucks. But once

the bucks are led about by hot does, all bets are off. Deer movement becomes helter-skelter. An oak ridge torn up with deer sign one day can be void of deer the next. One doe in heat can pull in bucks from a wide surrounding area to challenge for the right to breed her. That means that you can be in the middle of the mayhem or on an island of trees, squirrels and jays.

Give up the rut? Never. The payoff is enormous. It's like playing the lotto when the jackpots get really high. The odds of winning become even more astronomically low, but the dream makes you play. Early-season hunting lacks the frenzy, but I like the odds better.

STACKING THE DECK

Okay, so I say you can't effectively pattern mature early-season bucks. Then how do we decide where to hunt? First, don't misunderstand. Though I don't believe that you can truly pattern a buck in the strictest sense of the word, you can gain some important information by scouting from a distance before the season begins. It makes sense to watch fields and talk to postal carriers, bus drivers and others who spend time out and about near your hunting area. Any information is better than nothing. But I believe it boils down to this: Hunt the feed and do everything in your power to avoid

Thick early-season foliage makes it easier to hide from a whitetail's eyesight. But you have to consider stand positioning and shooting lanes to make sure you have a clear alley toward passing deer.

detection by the deer.

Here's what I mean. Say you've been watching a handful of whitetails feeding in a nearby alfalfa field in the evenings. You've seen them emerge from the woods from primarily two locations and you think that you can hang a stand close to both spots. In my opinion this scenario allows you one mistake. You can get caught in one stand, but if you're busted in both you'll not kill a good buck on that field during the pre-rut. Same goes for an apple orchard, oak grove, whatever. A mistake during the rut does not have the consequences that it does during the early season.

Thus, you need options. You know where to expect the deer to come from. You know where they'll be at dark. If the wind is going to cause you serious problems, you cannot hunt that stand. You also must put that stand in a place where you have a chance to kill passing deer but can access and exit the stand without giving the tree away to the deer.

If I happen to bump a deer 100 yards from my tree, that's one thing. Having one catch me *in* the tree means that spot's going to be tough.

Most hunters, I think, believe that mature bucks are mostly nocturnal early in the season because of warm temperatures. But while deer will certainly move mostly at the edge of daylight early in the season, all whitetails, even older bucks, will show themselves during legal shooting light from time to time if you're in the right location.

Soft-mast food sources like apples and other fruits can be early-season whitetail magnets.

EARLY TO BED

Hunting early-season whitetails in the morning means setting up away from the feeding areas. You can't expect to get to a field-edge treestand undetected in the morning. Before the season you should have located deer trails from the feed to likely bedding areas. Try to find a location closer to the bedding area in hopes of catching the deer on their way back to bed.

The success of your morning hunts might depend a lot on the weather and the moon. If it's dark and cold or rainy at night, the odds of deer staying out to feed later in the morning are better. Bright, clear, warm nights generally mean that deer might be bedded before daylight.

But remember, you can't kill one unless you're out there. Better to hunt, provided the wind is in your favor. Also, just as you can't expect to sneak in close to feeding areas for a morning hunt, you can't expect to exit your stand without detection if you're right on the brush where the deer will bed. Give yourself an out so that if the deer pass out of range, or you pass on some does in the morning, you can get out of your stand and back home for breakfast undetected.

EARLY TO RISE?

Don't count on it. Early-season afternoon hunts are generally about the last half-hour of daylight. Again, I think you're better off between the bed and the feed instead of right on it, but it's often difficult to hunt inside the woods early in the season. Thick foliage and a variety of trails mean that the deer might slip by unnoticed. You can certainly hunt the field edges where the trails converge, but slipping out discreetly in the dark is often tricky. And if you want to lose a buck until the rut, stepping on him early in the season is a good way to do it.

If you're going to hunt right on the field, get up high in a tree that offers good concealment. Don't go higher than you're comfortable, but many veteran deer hunters I know like stands that are at least 20 feet off the ground. These stands keep you out of sight better and give you better odds of avoiding a deer's nose. Trim necessary branches so that you can shoot to a couple of likely spots, but keep as much natural cover surrounding you as possible as long as it doesn't inhibit your movement.

EARLY-SEASON REWARDS

Early-season whitetail hunting requires stealth. It means dealing with uncomfortably warm weather and bothersome insects. But even if you don't tag your deer early in the season, you will be far ahead by the time the rut rolls around. You'll know the deer in your area that much better. Where they like to travel and when. Which oaks they've been hitting. How they've been using the standing corn. You might also get to look over some of the bucks in your area. In fact, if you see one, you're likely to see most of them, since they'll often be found in bachelor groups until the rut nears. And if you do everything right, you'll sneak into your stand mid-afternoon one September day, watch a couple of does and fawns amble by and then, just as the last rays of light slash into the western sky, draw your bow on an old short-haired, slick-coated buck headed for the field. In those states with a one-buck limit you'll miss the rut, but I don't think you'll care when you're attaching your tag to him.

Early-season deer hunting is often a dawn to dusk proposition, as warm temperatures might suppress midday deer movement.

September Western Success

Actually, it was August. The last day of August in Idaho. And the conditions couldn't have been worse for an early-season bowhunt. Daytime highs pushed into the upper 90s, and it hadn't rained in weeks. If I were at home facing similar early-season conditions, I might well have waited for a break in the weather. But when you travel halfway across the country and have a nonresident tag in your pocket, you hunt. So that's what I did, and what a hunt it was.

Tim Craig owns Boulder Creek Outfitters and understands how his mountain whitetails use the habitat. Most of his treestands are set along well-worn trails on the sides of steep, grassy hills dotted with pines and pockets of heavy brush. More importantly, you'll find within bow range of most of those stands native, wild fruit trees bearing apples, pears and plums. The deer gravitate to these soft-mast food sources as they move between bedding areas and the fields of alfalfa and other agricultural crops below.

In fact, the hot, dry weather might have actually improved the activity around these soft-mast food sources since the deer were likely drawing significant amounts of needed water from the juicy fruits. By the second afternoon of the hunt, I'd seen countless whitetails stand nearby happily mashing apple after apple in their mouths. Some individual deer spent nearly half an hour at a tree with a lot of fruit. Though most of the deer were does and fawns, I spotted three mature bucks and killed the third one that second day.

True to form, the buck was the last whitetail to trot down the hillside trail that evening, with just minutes of shooting light remaining. He stood up high and scanned the apple tree suspiciously from approximately 100 yards away until he was satisfied that the coast was clear. With the wind in my face and the stand a good 25 feet up in a thick pine, all I had to do was make the 25-yard broad-

The author with an August 31st Idaho whitetail taken near an apple tree.

side shot. I don't know if I'll ever kill another whitetail on a hotter day or in the month of August for that matter. But I'm sure glad I was there to learn how important soft mast can be early in the season.

MONTANA

Three weeks later I still couldn't escape the heat in southeastern Montana. I'd heard about the riverbottom whitetail hunting in Big Sky Country, and finally had the opportunity to sample it with Doug Gardner's Powder River Outfitters based in the scenic country near Broadus.

Riverbottom Western whitetails are very predictable in their travels. Even so, stand placement has to be precise in order to connect.

Mule deer and whitetails intermingle a bit on the ranches that Doug leases along the Powder River, but for the most part the whitetails stick to the cottonwood-lined river while the mulies prefer the mountains a mile or so off the river banks.

Again, it's an early-season matter of feed and cover for the whitetails. Adjacent to the riverbottoms are irrigated fields of alfalfa that feed the sheep and cattle raised by local ranchers. And heavy brush in some areas of the riverbottom provide the necessary security for whitetail bedding areas.

But it was hot. This time well into the 80s during midday, 60s in the morning when we climbed into an old cottonwood not 100 yards from the Powder River. Just before shooting light that first morning, I saw two fine whitetailed bucks pass on a trail about 70 yards out and scoot across a sage flat to the brush where Doug said the deer were bedding. He'd been watching the deer with binoculars for the past few days and knew that they were traveling nearly two miles from their preferred bedding spot to a lush alfalfa field to the north.

The next hour was a constant parade of whitetails, none within bow range, but all within clear view in the open riverbottom country. I didn't keep an exact count, but I'll estimate that I saw 20 to 25 deer, five of which were mature bucks 2½ years old or older.

Doug knew that this stand location was our only legitimate shot for a morning stand given the terrain and hunting conditions. The field where the deer were feeding was far enough away from the stand site so that we could slip in under the cloak of darkness and have a chance of the deer not getting to us until we had enough light to videotape.

Evening stands were easier, as long as we had a way to get out at dark without busting all the deer out feeding. Doug kept these considerations in mind, and we played the wind from there. During the five-day hunt I lost count of the number of good bucks that I saw. And on the last morning, from the same cottonwood where I started my hunt, I killed a wide 9-point. In fact, I recognized him as the same buck I'd seen two days earlier. That day he was the last in a string of nine racked bachelor-group bucks that passed just outside of bow range.

The last morning, rain and fog kept him out feeding later, and he was separated from his buddies. Instead of taking the same out-of-range trail that they followed, he headed right for our tree and turned out into the sage flat upwind of us. Sometimes, it pays to be a little bit lucky on whitetails.

But again, we made our luck by playing the hand we were dealt and not letting the weather discourage us. The deer still need to eat. And that is your main consideration in attempting to take an early-season whitetail, west or east.

GUN SEASON

In the state where I grew up, the regular firearms deer season is nine days long. It was that way when I started deer hunting a couple of decades ago and it has never changed. During the years, the season length has been a point of contention. Some groups have argued that a 16-day season should be considered in order to help "spread out" the hunting pressure. But that suggestion has never flown with the majority of hunters.

It's easy to understand the reasoning of the hunters who like the nine-day format opening on a Saturday and ending the following Sunday. If they wish, they can take one week of vacation from their jobs and not miss a single day of hunting. That means someone else isn't getting opportunity that they can't enjoy.

Many of these same hunters also argue that exposing the whitetail herd to 16 days of firearms-hunting pressure would mean that tens of thousands of additional deer would be harvested. And that, they argue, could damage the overall health of the herd. The Department of Natural Resources doesn't necessarily agree that more days would result in a significant increase in the deer harvest. They know the harvest statistics during the firearms season and understand how dramatically it drops after 4:30 p.m. on the opening Saturday.

Gun hunters with access to private property have the advantage of hunting bucks that haven't been pushed to nocturnal activity by hunting pressure.

THE PRESSURE COOKER

As an example of the hunting pressure opening day can produce, approximately 700,000 hunters head afield each season for the Wisconsin gun deer season opener. By the end of the day, they'll harvest something like 100,000 deer. By the end of the nine days the total harvest will reach somewhere around 300,000. At least that's how it's gone on average during the past 10 to 15 years as the deer population has leveled off in the neighborhood of 1 million animals. That's an intense hunting scenario not unlike that seen in other states like Michigan, Pennsylvania and others.

Gun season is special. And though, to me, it is not the same tranquil experience that bowhunting brings, I wouldn't miss gun deer season for the world. Well, I missed it once when I had drawn one of the first Kansas deer tags ever available to a nonresident. With visions of record-book bucks dancing in my head, I drove to Kansas and came home five days later kicking myself for not going to our tiny cabin in

the northern forest of Wisconsin. Never again.

For many deer hunters, like my dad, the annual gun deer season is the only deer hunting of the year. I wish more hunters would try bowhunting or muzzleloading and extend their time afield, but on the other hand I clearly understand the commitments to family and job and the difficulty of getting away. So we have what we have with gun season. A fleeting few days oozing with tradition and anticipation. A deer herd in the midst of or just concluding rut activities. And dreams of a mature buck materializing in front of our stand in the early-morning light.

I've never killed a big buck during gun season, but I had a chance once when I was too young to take advantage of the slam-dunk opportunity in front of me. Since then, I've gun hunted mostly in the northern forest of Wisconsin where big-racked bucks are rare; does, spikes and basket-racked forks and 6-points have made up most of my gun season take. Still, I've learned a lot during gun seasons and covered a lot of ground trying to search out the secrets of how so many deer

In some locations, a treestand is an advantage for a gun hunter, but other times ground hunting offers more versatility and almost as much view of the forest. No matter what kind of stand you choose, stay alert, because a whitetail during gun season likely won't be in view for long.

elude so many hunters armed with the finest deer hunting rifles, optics and gear. How is it possible that only 30 percent of the hunters fill a tag, despite the fact that the deer herd is bulging at the seams?

They're whitetails. I guess it's as simple as that. I'm convinced that you could open a 16-day or 26-day gun deer season and still not negatively impact deer herds in most states. Whitetails are the most resourceful, adaptable big game creatures on this continent. The anti-hunters don't have to worry about protecting whitetails from over-hunting. The deer can do just fine by themselves, thank you.

So what separates the successful gun deer hunter from the majority of those who go home with unfilled tags? Well, obviously, there's no simple answer to that question. But I have some ideas about tactics that are important to remember come opening day of gun season.

CHOOSING AN OPENING DAY STAND

In nearly 20 years of deer hunting, I bet I've hunted 15 different opening day stands. I know other hunters, like my dad, who have spent most opening days on a single stand. I guess I'm still looking for that perfect place. Or maybe there's no such thing.

Calling and scents can lure in whitetails even during gun season. But after opening day, hunting pressure might make these methods useless.

Some of you reading this book might have access to a large piece of private property for the firearms deer season. Maybe it's a big farm covering more than a section of land. Or, if you live in the South, where deer seasons are much longer, hunting pressure might not be the same concern that it is in most states. But for the vast majority of deer hunters out there, success during the gun deer season is as much about reading the other hunters as it is reading the deer themselves.

Much of the deer movement you'll witness during gun season is the result of the deer being moved by hunters walking to and from stands, shooting at deer or making concert-

A common sight during gun season. Put yourself in the escape zones and you'll increase your odds for success.

ed deer drives. The exceptions are those cases mentioned above: sole access to a large chunk of private land; long gun deer seasons that reduce hunting pressure; and to a smaller degree, opening day. I've witnessed natural deer movement on opening day before the deer recognize what's going on around them.

Anticipating Some Natural Movement

This season past, I hung a treestand in the same tree as my brother, Jeff, and carried a video camera with me instead of my deer rifle. I get to hunt deer a lot, but don't get to hunt with my family nearly enough. So I chose to share the day with my brother. Right at first light on opening morning, I heard the sounds of a running deer tearing across the frosty leaves. Then, it sounded like two. At first I suspected they'd been bumped by another hunter walking to his stand, but just as I could make out their dark forms, I heard the grunts of a lovesick buck in pursuit of a doe. It was still too dark to search out open shooting lanes, and the deer were out too far and moving too fast for Jeff to take a reasonable shot. He hit his grunt call in an effort to stop the deer, but that doe wasn't stopping with that buck hot on her tail. They barreled across the flat and were gone into the cedar swamp. I'd bet that before the end of that day, if the buck were still alive, he'd have learned to keep his chasing to the nighttime hours.

A few years back, my brother, Scott, took a nice buck that came to check a scrape early on opening morning. Scott had doused the scrape with doe-in-heat scent and killed the buck before it had a chance to hear much opening-day gunfire.

Then there was a North American Hunting Club member in southern Minnesota who we taped during opening day of a recent gun season in that state. On videotape that hunter misses a buck four times before finally killing it with the fifth shot from his slug gun. And the deer never appeared to realize that it was being hunted. It's all on tape. The buck was right on the tail of what must have been a doe in heat, because he never breaks from his pursuit of the doe during all the shooting. This is an extraordinary case, to be sure. But it can happen this way, and for this reason, it makes sense to hunt opening day deer sign the same way you might if it were bow season or if you were the only hunter allowed in the woods. Feeding areas, rut sign and deer trails all hold some promise that first day.

Anticipating Hunter Movement

But many more of the bucks killed in our camp on opening day were already seeking sanctuary from the human intruders. In fact, the best buck ever taken in our camp had been shot at and missed before my friend, Terry Kisiolek, dropped him in mid-stride as the buck was on a mad dash for the cedar swamp tangle 100 yards distant. The massive 9-point scored something like 140 gross Boone and Crockett Club inches and was probably at least 4, maybe 5 years old. That buck had seen this thing before and knew he needed to find cover. But the buck chose his escape route a little too late, and Terry was waiting.

What kind of stand should you look for? Well, based on what my campmates and I have experienced on the public land where we deer hunt, I'd choose the escape routes over the scrapes, rubs or feeding areas. And I'd choose it right from the opening bell, especially if you have your sights set on a big buck. Like I said, yearling bucks might take longer to realize the error of their ways. Mature bucks have been there, done that. They hear those first few pickups bouncing along the logging road and they're going under cover.

PATTERNING HUNTERS

Where do the deer go? I wish I knew. My campmates and I pour over the same topographical maps every year the night before opener. And then we pour over them again at the end of the first day. We've memorized the ridges and creeks and logging trails; that doesn't change. But every year the gun hunting landscape changes because the hunting pressure changes.

All it takes to change the complexion of your own stand setup is one hunter setting up in a place you didn't expect. Some years we have pickup loads of hunters at the end of our favorite logging trail. Other years, no one. And that has a dramatic impact on what the deer do—especially on opening day.

Hunting pressure will dictate how the deer move during gun season more than food or rut. The deer will tend to those things after nightfall when things quiet down. And you'll walk to your stand each day wondering where all the deer are that are making all the fresh tracks. So, where will the other hunters be? Where will they park? How will they walk to their stands? What are the natural barriers that will keep them out of certain areas?

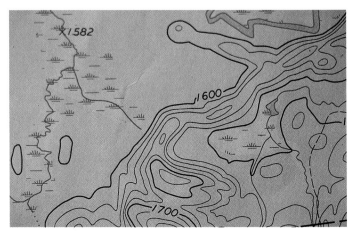

A topo map is almost as valuable at helping you determine where hunters are likely to be as it is for determining where deer are likely to be.

These are things you cannot see on the section of land around you, but they are things that you can make an educated guess about given a good topographical map. I've often thought that one of the most valuable things I could do on an opening day would be to ride around in my pickup and note where other hunters are parked. By driving every logging road in my area, and mapping out every parked vehicle, I think I could do a pretty fair job of assessing where the various hunters are located. So far, I haven't had the nerve to lose an opening day on stand in favor of sitting in my pickup. Someday, though, I'll do it.

Will you spot him before he spots you? Or are you better off staying on stand and allowing other hunters to bump deer and move them past you?

Better yet, I've also thought of renting an airplane (pilot supplied, of course) for an hour or two of opening day airtime above the forest where I deer hunt. Imagine being able to have a bird's-eye view of the hunting pressure over square miles of country. Imagine also the opportunity to see deer heading for solitude or congregated in particular areas.

Granted, in wooded country you can't see everything. The cedars and balsams where I hunt would hide a lot of the deer and some of the deer hunters, but I'd bet that on a day with good snow cover, I'd be able to spot a lot of the blaze orange from the air.

I'll also grant you this. I did say that the hunting pressure changes from year to year. However, my main objective from the sky would be to search out areas that other hunters have *not* penetrated. Places farther from the logging roads or places guarded by creeks or other obstacles to a deer hunter on foot. No such place, you say? Well, I'll admit that most of the big forest that I hunt has seen some deer hunting pressure. But I'll bet that from the sky I could get a much better picture of high-percentage, low-pressure places to set up.

I've also heard the argument that deer don't necessarily leave their home ranges, despite pressure from hunters. The argument is that going farther than the next hunter isn't always the answer. And I'll agree with that as well. Maybe I'd see from the sky that there appears to be a great escape route very close to a logging road and that nobody is hunting there. I'm not necessarily looking for the most impenetrable swamp or the highest mountain. I'm just looking for vacant areas that I think deer would seek out.

The All-Day Hunt

In Chapter 1 you found a sidebar titled, "Does Midday Really Pay?" That piece focused on natural midday deer movement that has the most meaning for bowhunters. Firearms season is different. We all know that once the hunting pressure starts, most deer movement is going to occur at night. And since after opening day most daytime deer movement is going to be hunter-induced, hunter movement times are deer movement times. That means early, middle and late.

I'll wager that most of the deer killed on opening day fall during the first hour of legal shooting light. You have a couple of converging factors in your favor. Deer have been out rutting or feeding since they've curbed most daytime travel. Depending on the weather and other factors, they might be still on their feet after shooting light arrives. In addition, there are always some hunters getting to the woods late, walking to stands after legal shooting light. It pays to be on your stand well in advance (I'd say 20 minutes or so) before legal shooting light.

By late morning, a lot of hunters have had enough. They're cold, hungry, nature's calling or the couch and the football game are beckoning. Deer have a lot more discipline than most deer hunters. Some hunters might not leave the woods altogether but choose instead to still-hunt for a while to warm up or see some new surroundings. All this move-

ment can mean deer movement. Again, I'll say that it pays to stay on stand all day if possible. The still-hunter is more likely to move a deer to you than to kill one himself.

Later on into midday (early afternoon) a lot of hunters start filtering back to stands. This is another opportunity for deer sightings. And so are those final precious minutes of legal shooting light. Like the early-morning hunt, you have deer that are starting to stand from beds and think about feeding or rutting. You also have a lot of hunters bolting for the pickup before legal shooting time actually ends. Either factor can play to your hand if you'll stay put until legal shooting time has come to an end.

Bucks will still work scrapes and exhibit rutting behavior during gun season, but a lot of it will probably happen under the cloak of darkness.

If you leave the woods during legal shooting hours, be on alert. A deer can cross your path at any moment.

This is all easier said than done, and I'll admit that I don't stay on stand all day, every day. If you prepare for it, however, it can be done in relative comfort. Other chapters of this book will outline clothing and other gear that will help you get through the day. But suffice it to say that the most important ingredients are a good lunch, quality clothing, a bottle to urinate in and toilet paper, so that you don't have to leave the woods entirely if nature calls. Some hunters take a paperback book, read a page and scan the woods for a few minutes before starting on the next page. It would be better to concentrate entirely on your surroundings, of course, but staying on stand, even if it means that your eyes are on the pages of a book some of the time, is better than leaving early.

MOVING DEER WHEN THEY WON'T MOVE

In Chapter 4 of this book you'll find a section titled, "The Deer Drive." It merits mention here because, despite all the advice you've read about locating high-percentage stand sites and putting in hours on stand, one well-planned deer drive can move more deer by you than you might see in two or three days of solid stand sitting.

I won't steal that section's thunder here, but later in any gun deer season, deer drives or "pushes" make sense. Even in the unbroken forest where our deer camp is located, we've had excellent success moving deer to particular locations even with only a couple of drivers on foot. For more on this tactic, see Chapter 4.

The gun hunter who can find the sanctuaries and use other hunters to his advantage is the one who consistently notches his tag.

LATE SEASON

Maybe you're a bowhunter with an unfilled tag. Maybe a muzzleloader hunter whose season is just beginning. No matter. When you find yourself in pursuit of white-tailed deer after the regular firearms season has passed, you find yourself in the most challenging of all deer hunting.

A TOUGH HUNT

By the time the regular firearms season has ended in most states where whitetails live, the deer have been pressured for two months or more by human hunters. In the North they've also gone through the rigors of the rut and all the physical drains that the breeding season brings with it. For the males of the species, it has been an especially trying couple of months.

Naturally, bucks are targeted more aggressively by hunters and they face the very real danger of being gored and even killed by competitors during the rut. If they've survived it all, including an intense firearms season, they are survivors in every sense of the word. Killing a whitetail during the late season requires a heightened level of dedication.

Late-season deer hunting is rarely fun. Where I'm from it is downright cold, and if it's not, it's not worth hunting anyway because the deer hunting isn't any good unless it's cold enough to make you miserable after an hour in a stand. Rattling and grunting draw little response and might actually turn a weary buck in the other direction. Scrapes are filling with snow or leaves, bright rubs are fading and losing their luster. The corn or beans are plowed under, acorns are rapidly disappearing, and it's difficult to decipher where the deer are feeding and when. Sightings decrease, and what few deer you do see are traveling only on the very edge of darkness after so much pressure from hunters. Yes, late season lacks a great deal in the excitement category. But you have two options

Muzzleloader season often occurs after the regular firearm hunt, meaning that deer have been exposed to a couple months of hunting pressure.

during the late season: Hunt, or stay home and dream of next season by the fireplace.

If you want to go hunting, come along the rest of the way through this section and we'll see if we can't put you on a whitetail before the clock runs out.

It's All About Food

We stressed food sources when we talked about early-season deer hunting. You should realize by now that feeding areas are always an important consideration. But there is no more important time to target food than during the late season. Given the stresses of the rut and hunting seasons now passed, the local whitetails that are left must gain back important fat reserves lost during the past month. To fail means death across the northern reaches of the deer's range. In fact, it's not uncommon for tens of thousands of deer to die in states like Minnesota, Wisconsin and Michigan during a severe winter.

Forage is everything, and not just in the north. Even in the South deer must concentrate on feed. Does need it to maintain their unborn fetuses through winter, and bucks must come through winter in decent shape if they're going to survive to compete for breeding rights the following fall. And in the wild, passing along genetics is the driving force.

Reason for Optimism

I have a friend in Kansas, Sam Lancaster, who owns Claythorne Lodge near Columbus, in the southeastern portion of this fantastic whitetail hunting state. Sam is one of five owners in a choice 1,220-acre piece of deer hunting real estate. He and his partners put in a lot of hours in treestands from the start of the bow season right up until the final day.

And though the rut is often heated and exciting on the property, Sam likes his odds during the late season after gun season has closed. There are a couple of very good reasons for his optimism about bowhunting in December and January.

One centers on the fact that he and his partners don't hunt their piece during gun season. Thus, a lot of deer from

Food sources are never more crucial than during the late season. The more bitter the weather, the better the hunting.

It's easy to spot late-season food sources. Tracks will be abundant as deer compete for what's left.

SETTLING BACK IN

While Sam's experience serves as a fine example of the food factor during the late season, you might be saying that you don't have the luxury of your own late-season deer haven. Maybe you hunt public property or a private place that got hunted hard by some other hunters during gun season. Not many of us have exclusive use of deer hunting land from opening to closing.

But I'll almost guarantee you that you won't see many hunters out after the final day of the regular gun season. That's certainly an advantage. It might take a couple of weeks for the deer to settle back into a pattern, but if the pressure lightens and you don't force the issue, you'll likely notice that the deer will be up and moving later into the morning and again earlier in the afternoons to get back out to feed. They have to eat. It's your job to figure out where, and then not to get caught.

More pressure at this point in the season will only help to turn the deer to more night-time activity. You can make a small mistake early in the season because the deer haven't been bothered for a number of months. And you've got the upcoming rut and gun season in your back pocket. But if you muck it up during the late season, it's over for eight or nine months.

HUNT THE FEED—AND THE TRAILS TO IT

If you've done your homework and scouted properly, you should know the forage options available to the deer. Go midday, get in and get back out again. You'll know the spot when you see it. It'll likely be trampled with tracks and pawed whether the whitetails are searching out acorns, winter wheat, or unharvested corn or beans. Because food sources are depleted during the late season, whitetails tend to congregate close to what's left. That means you'll likely see numbers of deer or none at all.

If you're hunting with a muzzleloader, you have the luxury of staying farther away from the food and reducing the odds of being smelled or seen. Bow-hunters are better served by seeking out the main trail leading to the feed and playing the wind. Once deer get to the feed and are all standing still scanning for danger in every direction, it's going to be

There's no mistaking where they're coming from and where they're going. Now you just have to find a spot where the deer will show up during legal shooting light.

surrounding properties are pushed in. And when they get there the deer have every reason to stay. Sam has planted six food plots totalling about 5 acres around the property. A plant called "rappa," a leafy lettuce-like plant is Sam's favorite, and the deer pour into these food plots late in the season. In fact, Sam has seen some Boone and Crockett Club-class bucks feeding in the food plots during December and January.

"During the rut is still a super time, but I'm not worried about holding out until late season," Sam says. "I'm so busy (at the lodge) in November, that I don't get much of a chance to bowhunt until December. And that's when those deer really hit that rappa."

Even in the South, late-season hunts revolve around food. Does need the nutrition to give birth to healthy fawns.

extremely difficult to get your bow drawn, no matter how good your blind or how high your treestand.

On the other hand, trail hunting allows you to let non-target deer pass and gives you better odds of dealing with a single deer at a time. I've already preached the merits of high treestands, but it bears repeating here because again we're talking about pressured deer that might have encountered people at the 10- to 15-foot level already this season. Another 10 feet might make the difference during the late season. And given the more open nature of the winter woods, height is often the only way to improve your odds of not being seen. Pines and other evergreens are always good choices if they're within bow range of a promising trail, but they're especially important when the leaves are down. Lacking these evergreens, opt for a thick-trunked tree if at all possible to help break your outline.

THE LATE SEASON DOWN SOUTH

At the beginning of this piece on late season hunting, I talked about the challenges of late-season whitetail hunting when the rut occurs before the firearms season and the bow or muzzleloader seasons remain.

But in the South, the late-season scenario might actually occur in the middle of the season. Here's what I mean: In states like Alabama the rut might not occur until the very end of the hunting season, late in December and well into January. The regular firearms season is in November. So December, after a month of bowhunting and a couple of weeks of gun season, is the challenging time for the Southern deer hunter who's still waiting for the rut to roll around.

"They go back to the thickest, most inaccessible stuff they can find," says well-known deer hunter and videographer Ron Jolly. "We have a long deer season, and after about two weeks of that rifle hunting, they've been kicked around quite a bit. In the month of December, if you see one of those son of a guns, you kicked him out of his bed."

Jolly said that the rut often seems more spread out in the South and that it can even extend into February in some regions. That means that the "late" season is really the best season in some regions of the whitetail's range.

However, there are stretches in the South where the rut does wind down weeks before the season actually closes. And Jolly says that where that is the case, just like in the North, food sources become the primary places to stake out.

"If there are still acorns, that's a great place, but normally there are not that many left," Jolly says. "If you can find any planted green plots, especially for afternoon hunts, those can be full of deer. Our deer really focus too, on greenbriar and dewberry briar. They really like to hit that browse at that time."

SOME GOOD NEWS: NORTH

Though I painted a bleak picture at the outset of this section, late-season hunting is not entirely without advantages.

Bucks have burned fat reserves while eluding hunters and battling for breeding rights. The onset of cold means eat or die.

In the North, of course, there is the very likely snow scenario. That means that it's easier to find sign. It also means an easier time of deciphering that sign on a day-to-day basis as the snow pack changes. Because food sources are dwindling and whitetails are congregating heavily at favored feeding areas, one field or acorn ridge might dry up in a matter of days. It's not like September, when the whitetails stepped out into a sea of lush alfalfa. You'll have to be mobile and stay on top of the sign.

And when the whitetails do find something to their liking, don't be surprised if they don't stray too far away to bed. Every step means energy. Energy requires nutrients. Fewer steps means more calories stored for fat that might mean sur-

vival through the winter or another fawn born in the spring. And with food and bed close together, it's easy to misstep.

"When you're dealing with post-rut, those big deer are the most prolific breeders and they're run down and gotta eat; it's that simple," says veteran deer hunter and author Greg Miller. "But the desire to eat (during the day) is greatly influenced by weather. The last week of the season a couple of years ago I killed a Pope and Young-class buck, and it was definitely weather influenced."

PREVENTING EQUIPMENT FAILURE

I'll wager that equipment failure is a bugaboo for a lot of late-season deer hunters. In the case of bowhunters, your gear has gone through a couple months of wear and tear. Conscientious bowhunters take care of string wear and keep an eye on their arrow rests and nock sets. Still, most hunters don't spend as much time, if any, at the practice range anymore during this part of the season. It's getting colder after all, and the days are shorter. Everything was in working order and shooting fine a month ago, so what could go wrong?

Plenty.

If you're going to suffer the blustery weather and challenge yourself against late-season deer, you must take stock of your equipment—namely, your bow or muzzleloader. Cold weather means creaky, icy treestands. It can cause a squeak in what used to be a whisper-quiet bow. And in the case of a muzzleloader, cold in the deer woods and warm in the house means the potential for condensation and moisture. And moisture and blackpowder or Pyrodex don't mix.

To you bowhunters: Spend time at the range practicing late in the season. And try drawing your bow one day after an hour of sitting still in a cold treestand. You might find that the bow's draw weight has to be turned down because of your extra clothing and tightened muscles. You'll also notice if your bow sounds any different when it's 20°F instead of 45°F. If everything's in order, you'll go to the woods with more confidence.

You need the mental toughness to hunt the late season, but you also need equipment that's tough enough to withstand the conditions.

Dressing for Success

L ate-season hunting means colder temperatures. And even if you're hunting in the South in January it can be downright cold on stand for hours at a time.

The most important layer of clothing for any late-season hunter is the one that he puts right next to his skin. A material that is going to wick moisture away from your skin is absolutely essential if you want to stay warm and comfortable. Polypropylene is popular. I have some Cabela's PolarTec insulated underwear that is lightweight and does a great job of keeping moisture from sweat away from my body.

From there it comes down to layering. Shirts, vests and jackets with Gore's Windstopper membrane are excellent, but wool is still an excellent performer that has stood the test of time. As an outer layer, wool does a decent job of repelling rain and snow. And it's super quiet. If you're expecting heavy snow or rain, or even if you're not, for that matter, it's always wise to carry a quiet, lightweight set of raingear that you can pull over the top of everything. If you get wet, your hunt is soon over.

Knee-high rubber boots are my choice for a lot of my deer hunting, but they generally don't cut it during late-season, despite some models now available with 1,000 grams of Thinsulate insulation. Pac boots with thick felt liners are a better choice and are fine unless you have a very long walk to your stand. If that's the case, I recommend you wear lighter footwear and switch when you get to your stand, or invest in a pair of the boot blankets available at sporting goods stores.

My hands don't do well in the cold, but they do better now that I wear a handwarmer muff about my waist. You've seen football players tuck their hands in a muff between plays; I keep my hands inside until I spot a deer. Then I quietly slip them out to grab my bow or gun from the hook. With a couple of chemical handwarmers inside, my hands are good for an all-day sit. And I don't need bulky mittens or really thick gloves that always get in the way whether you're hunting with a bow or gun.

The bottom line is to make sure not to overdress for the walk into your stand. You don't need many layers while you're walking. Get a good-sized backpack and stuff extra layers inside. Dress a few minutes *after* arriving at your stand and cooling down. If you sweat on the way in, you're in trouble even with good wicking underwear. From there, make sure that the hunting clothes that you choose are quiet and have good insulating qualities. Take extra care of your feet and hands. And top it off with a good stocking cap or hood to hold in the heat that is lost around your neck and head. Much body heat is lost right there.

And remember—you still have to be able to shoot. Practice drawing your bow or shouldering your rifle with all those clothes on and make sure that you'll be able to do it without excess movement or noise. If you're a bowhunter, a chest protector helps to pull in your jacket to keep it out of the way of your bowstring. For the same reason, an armguard is a necessity when you are wearing multiple layers of clothing.

Shooting stance is also a consideration. A more open stance with toes pointing more toward the target moves the bow arm and the chest out of the path of the bowstring. And that means accuracy won't be compromised by the string brushing clothing as it speeds forward. The result? Better chances of you notching your tag with a late-season whitetail.

A handwarmer seems like an insignificant piece of equipment, but it can mean another hour or two on stand. And that can be the difference.

Chapter 3

THE RUT

Pressure. Two weeks or so, and it's gone. The whitetail rut is what our dreams are made of. We wait for it. We plan for it. And, if we're lucky (and good), our dreams of a giant buck come true.

One thing's for certain. Though we might not convince you in this book to suffer through the chill and challenge of the late season; though you might not look forward to the mosquitoes and heat of the early season; you better log your hours during the rut. At least if you have dreams of witnessing white-tailed deer hunting at its wildest.

But it's no sure thing, this whitetail rut. We make that point clearly a number of times. In fact, this might be one of the most challenging times to predict when and where a buck will show. But your odds of seeing deer, including those ghostly old, hunt-wise bucks, are never better than now.

In this chapter we'll address the decisions that factor into your rut-hunting strategy. We'll try to get a feel for when the rut is most likely to occur. We'll address rut sign, like scrapes and rubs. We'll get into the Xs and Os of decoying, calling and rattling. We'll analyze, calculate and plot along with some of the most veteran, knowledgeable deer hunters in the country, who'll join the rut-hunting discussion.

And then we'll go our separate ways to put it all to work, with dreams of the biggest buck we've ever laid eyes on slinking into the clear at 20 steps. It can happen. Especially during the rut.

PERFECT TIMING

*I*n the introduction to this book, I told you that my most important measure for hunting whitetails successfully is time in the deer woods. In fact, I mocked reliance on deer activity charts and other indicators that are supposed to help us choose which days and times to hunt. I stand by all of that and say that you are far better off hunting deer whenever you possibly can, rather than only on those days when deer movement is "supposed to be" good. Especially during the rut.

In this section, though, I will share a lot of information from a man I hold in high regard when it comes to matters of the white-tailed deer. And a lot of the information might

give you the idea that I am straying from my premise of diligent hunting over shortcut hunting. But I think that my friend, Charlie Alsheimer, quoted extensively in this section, will agree with my foundation for successful deer hunting, regardless of his extraordinary insights into white-tailed deer rut behavior.

Charlie is a deer hunter, photographer, writer and, recently, an avid deer researcher. In fact, he and his son, Aaron, have constructed a 35-acre high-fenced deer enclosure on their property in New York state in order to learn more about the animals that so fascinate them. As a result of this observation and a fair share of consultation with other prominent deer researchers, Charlie has reached some important conclusions about timing the deer rut in the North.

Time vs. timing; they're both important, of course. We deer hunters don't want to turn our backs on information that can benefit us with regard to timing, but we don't want to pin our hopes entirely on a small timeframe. So consider this enlightening information and use it if you wish to target your rut-hunting this season. But remember that as predictable as whitetails might be outside of the rut, they're equally unpredictable when the urge to procreate is the most important force in their lives.

RIGHT ON CUE: THE MOON

Alsheimer has a number of deer in his 35-acre enclosure and has been paying particular attention to three does for the past couple of years. While he admits that the photoperiod (or the decreasing amount of daylight) has a great deal to do with setting the stage for does to come into estrus, Alsheimer says that there is a second "cueing device" that has to kick in. That, he says, is the moon.

"They [the three does] are cycling right off what I call the hunter's moon, which is the second full moon after the autumn equinox," Alsheimer says. "The first full moon after the equinox is the harvest moon and the third one is the yule moon. Breeding occurs on all three."

Before continuing, we should point out that Alsheimer's names for the various full moons might not match what many of you are familiar with. Many people refer to the November full moon as the harvest moon. Alsheimer follows the naming given by an astronomy publication. The names don't really matter. Just remember the order and that the hunter's moon, the second one after the first day of fall, is the one that Alsheimer says cues up to 80 percent of the whitetail breeding activity any given season.

In an attempt to choose vacation days for an out-of-state or stay-at-home rut hunt, hunters have been trying to learn what cues the rut. It appears that rut timing might change year-to-year depending on the moon.

Technically speaking, bucks are ready for breeding as soon as they shed antler velvet. However, according to Charles Alsheimer, does aren't ready until photoperiod and the hunter's moon trigger the majority of the estrous cycle.

"Ten percent of the breeding is from the harvest moon (first full moon after the autumn equinox), 70 to 80 percent from the hunter's (second), then 10 percent from the yule," Alsheimer says.

DEFINING PEAK BREEDING TIME

Given the variance in full moon dates, the peak of the breeding around the hunter's moon could occur in the North anywhere from October 20, through November 25. So if Alsheimer is right, this would run counter to many deer hunters' and deer biologists' beliefs that the bulk of the breeding occurs around a certain date in specific areas regardless of moon, weather or other factors. And that would be the case if the breeding were dictated exclusively by the photoperiod.

The amount of daylight begins decreasing noticeably in September and drops to a point in late October and early November in the North when only about 11 hours of daylight remain. But then it flattens out. Alsheimer is convinced

that the moon effects the final change in white-tailed does to cause them to come into heat.

"It doesn't happen right when the full moon occurs," Alsheimer says. "Two days before the hunter's moon we are finding that these bucks are going into a frenzy. They go after every doe they can find. But the does have a physiological change in their system when that full moon hits and then they start to cycle.

"Some come in three days after the full moon and some not until a week after the moon. The breeding window is roughly two weeks long. When that last quarter phase hits after the hunter's moon, breeding has begun and scraping almost ceases."

A MAGIC WEEK?

Alsheimer says that if he had to pick one week of vacation for rut-hunting whitetails in the North, it would begin on the day of the hunter's moon and last for six days more.

Though this information might have you circling dates on the calendar with visions of big bucks dancing in your head, Alsheimer quickly points out that there are external factors that can impact the amount of deer movement you'll witness even if you target the hunter's moon.

Buck-to-doe ratio and the make-up of the local deer herd impacts the rut intensity. A tighter buck-to-doe ratio means more mature bucks, more intense competition and, likely, more daytime deer movement. Beyond that, Alsheimer says that not all hunter's moons are created equal.

"It's my belief that when the hunter's moon falls in the first week of November, the rut has the potential of being more intense than one in late October or mid- to late November," Alsheimer says. "Our research has shown that when the hunter's moon falls in late October or mid-November, there seems to be a bit of a trickle pattern to the rut, meaning it's less intense."

WEATHER MATTERS

Then there's the all-important weather. How many times have you planned for a week or long weekend of exciting rut hunting action only to be hit with unseasonably high temperatures? Does the heat push back the rut? Does weather play a role in actually determining when breeding will occur?

"Air temperature during the hunter's moon period is one thing that can never be predicted," Alsheimer says. "It's been my experience that for northern whitetails to be active during daylight hours, the air temperature needs to be less than 55°F. If the temperature tops 55°F, bucks tend to become inactive because they cannot handle the heat due to their thick winter coat. When temperatures exceed this mark, bucks will do nearly all their rutting behavior under the cover of darkness. Consequently, hunters might find incredible rut sign but see no deer. Probably nothing destroys hunting the rut more than high temperatures."

You'll notice that Alsheimer did not say that higher than normal temperatures will delay the rut. He believes that the rut goes on despite the weather but that we hunters don't get to witness a lot of it when it's warm.

Small waterholes or streams are places to consider during the rut. With all the chasing going on, deer need water more often—especially if temperatures are above normal.

Other researchers like Grant Woods, who has published articles in *North American Hunter* magazine on this topic, have also attempted to pin down deer activity. However, Woods's efforts have not been focused entirely on rut dates. His Deer Activity Index or DAI attempts to predict deer movement throughout hunting seasons from September through January.

YOU STILL HAVE TO HUNT HARD

It's up to you to decide how much stock you want to put in their findings. As I've pointed out earlier in this book, if you have one week of vacation time to dedicate to deer hunting around the rut, there's nothing wrong with targeting the dates that these researchers think give you the best odds for success. In fact, it's a wise move. Where some deer hunters go wrong, I think, is when they forsake other deer hunting opportunities on days early or late in the season because of an overreliance on the rut and, more specifically, a small window of dates within the rut timeframe. Hunt smart, and hunt long. Especially during the rut.

In regions with tight buck-to-doe ratios and a good age structure—including a fair percentage of bucks three years old and older—the rut can be fierce. These locations are where bucks have to fight for the right to breed.

South of the 40th

Those of you south of the 40th parallel reading this book are probably wondering why this section, "Perfect Timing," concentrates only on the North. The answer is that we don't have very good information on Southern rut timing.

Even though Southern rut dates can vary widely, many parts of the South do have a distinct rut—especially those places with a well-managed herd.

As you get closer to the equator, the rut becomes much more unpredictable because of the increased amount of daylight. Thus, with the photoperiod playing less of an influence, peak rut dates across the South can vary wildly compared to the North. And the moon seems to play an insignificant role. Different states in the South, even those in close proximity to one another, might have rut dates separated by a month or more. Even within individual states like Louisiana and Alabama we see widely ranging rut dates.

Why? Well, Charlie Alsheimer, who shed light on the influence of the moon in the North, thinks that the Southern rut is affected by a variety of factors like genetics, nutrition, buck-to-doe ratio and, to a lesser degree, the moon.

Decades ago, some Southern states restocked their whitetail herds with whitetails from Wisconsin. An earlier breeding date in those restocked areas might be a function of the genetics from those transplanted deer. Nutrition is important because does that are malnourished will not cycle predictably. Thus, the rut can be dragged out over a period of months. Buck-to-doe ratio is proven to have an impact and can even alter rut dates in the North. Generally speaking, the tighter the buck-to-doe ratio, the earlier the rut within a certain latitude.

Ronnie "Cuz" Strickland with a nice Mississippi buck.

Deer researcher Grant Woods, who has written about his Daytime Activity Index in *North American Hunter* magazine, has studied whitetails at the Mount Holly Plantation in South Carolina. He observed the deer for a number of years and as the buck-to-doe ratio tightened, the rut dates moved up nearly a month—all the way to September 21! That's a full two months earlier than in other parts of South Carolina.

As you can see, the Southern rut is much less predictable than in the North. And that's another good reason for hunting whenever you can and as long as you can if you want to hunt whitetails successfully.

DO SCRAPES WORK?

ore has probably been written about the merits of scrape hunting than any other approach. Find a buck's scrape, the theory goes, and you have found him. Hunt near his scrape, and eventually you will kill him.

I've killed *one* buck as a direct result of locating his scrapes. One—despite sitting untold hours near smoking-hot scrapes, making my own mock scrapes and doctoring up others to try to lure a buck within range. One buck. And, oh, the hours I've gambled on scrape-hunting success. I'd like to have some of those hours back to do things a little differently. Live and learn.

SCRAPE HUNTING CAN WORK

I don't mean to come off totally against the concept. Most hunters can look at deer tracks or droppings and not tell for certain whether that sign was left by a buck or doe. I'd like to think that I can tell one from the other by its track or droppings, but I'm not going to bet the farm. A scrape on the other hand; that's a buck, all right. And the fact that he stood in that one spot and made a scrape there causes a lot of hunters to pin their hopes on that buck coming back eventually. Problem is, most times he doesn't; at least not during daylight hours.

But there was that one buck of mine a few years back in southern Minnesota. It was the day before Halloween, cold and windy. A friend and I found a deer trail leading out of a likely bedding area and marked with three fresh buck scrapes about 15 or 20 yards apart. I sat within bow range of the final scrape after dumping doe-in-heat scent along the trail and in the scrapes.

An hour or so later, the buck (I'm not positive, of course, that it was the same buck that had made the scrapes) appeared on the trail and nosed the ground investigating the doe-in-heat lure I'd dumped. Step by excruciating step he worked his way along the trail, hooked a branch here and there with his antlers and nosed and pawed each of the three scrapes.

The first scrapes of the season are the most reliable for hunters. Once bucks begin chasing does, rut hunting is a low-percentage game.

Just after he turned out of the final scrape and stood broadside, I buried an Easton 2317 in his heart. At the time, he was the best buck I had ever killed with my bow. So why should I be so negative about scrapes? Well, like I've said, there are all those days before and since that I stared at scrapes filling up with falling leaves never to be returned to. Part of it is certainly my own fault. I've probably relied on scrapes mostly at the wrong times.

HUNT SCRAPES WHEN THE TIME IS RIGHT (*FIRST SCRAPES ARE BEST*)

Throughout this book I've preached that hours on stand outweigh all the gee-whiz stuff that you'll find in most hunting magazines—or books, for that matter. But sitting day after day on a buck scrape is often a recipe for failure. If that scrape appears in a good travel corridor along a heavily used deer trail, great. Stay put, provided there are fresh tracks in the area each day. But if you find a buck scrape on a field edge or open ridge with no heavy sign in the immediate area, I'd recommend that you play your cards elsewhere, especially if the bucks have been scraping for weeks now.

First scrapes are the best scrapes when it comes to your odds of harvesting a buck over a scrape. Bucks begin making scrapes early in the pre-rut as a means of identifying themselves to other deer, bucks and does. These early scrapes are made in areas that bucks utilize during their daily travels to feed and bed. Thus, with the rut still weeks off, and the bucks not yet into chase mode where they are searching out recep-

tive does, the likelihood of a buck returning to "check" that scrape is rather good. However, it's quite possible that he will do so at night.

Recently I was hunting with Tom Indrebo's Bluff Country Outfitters in western Wisconsin. Tom is a diligent deer watcher who is especially intrigued by trophy bucks. In order to learn more about the local deer, Tom hangs CamTrakker motion-detecting cameras on many of the scrapes that he locates early in the season. Typically, in his country, these scrapes start appearing in early to mid-October. By the time I arrived to hunt on October 31, Tom had a pretty good pile of buck photos taken at scrapes. Approximately 80 percent of those were recorded at night. And the cameras recorded very few bucks at scrapes after October 25. This buck behavior has been recorded by others who have observed the behavior of captive whitetails.

LATE SCRAPES: NOT AS GOOD

I'm convinced that once white-tailed bucks begin chasing does, which occurs two weeks or so prior to the peak breeding date in most areas, all bets are off on scrapes. Bucks will continue making scrapes and might even tear up an existing scrape, but this is more a matter of convenience than a concerted effort on behalf of the buck. When he's alone he might work off some rut-induced energy or anxiety by pawing a scrape. But what he's really looking for are receptive does. He doesn't care about scrapes. He cares about breeding.

North American Hunter "Whitetails" columnist Larry

Weishuhn once quoted scrape research in one of his columns. That research project indicated that 69 percent of the scraping activity occurred during the six weeks prior to the peak breeding dates with the vast majority of that scrap-

Adding scent to natural scrapes can improve the odds of a buck returning to that location. Some hunters prefer buck urine for this tactic; others like to use a doe-in-heat scent.

ing happening during the two weeks before breeding. This research project was conducted in Minnesota, and also found that none of the scrapes initiated after November 7 were worked a second time. These findings seem to support the idea that scrapes are secondary to doe chasing as the rut nears.

I've watched bucks make scrapes haphazardly as they've gone about their travels. And I'm quite certain that the vast majority of the scrapes that any deer hunter finds in the woods are ripped open, urinated in and never returned to by that buck or any other buck for that matter.

To me, that means that the first scrape or two that I find in the fall will capture my attention and probably even cause me to hang a stand nearby for a day or two of dedicated hunting of that location. But after scrapes have been in the woods for a couple of weeks, I'm going to look for more sign in my hunting location than the mere existence of a scrape.

FAKE SCRAPES: DO THEY WORK?

If it's true that scrapes are so unreliable, why have we read so much about the effectiveness of mock scrapes? That's a wonderful question. Here's the best answer I can give you.

A deer hunter can put a mock scrape anywhere. That's important, because now you don't have to rely on locating a real scrape in a high-traffic area. You can hunt high-traffic areas and add a mock scrape if you like.

Why add a mock scrape at all? Because once the bucks begin chasing, all bets are off as to where they'll appear. They might take the trail, might not. Might stay in the thick stuff, might stand out in the wide open. A mock scrape serves a purpose similar to that of a decoy. It's visual. It's something that can help you position a buck where you can make a clean, killing shot.

Now before you run out and start making mock scrapes all around your stand, let me point out that I've never killed a buck in any of the 100 or so mock scrapes I've made. Maybe I'm doing it wrong. I've watched hunters on video offer mock scrape instruction. I've read about it in magazines.

I'll be frank, it isn't rocket science. It doesn't need to be fancy. All a mock scrape has to be is visible, and positioned under an overhanging

Mock scrapes have to be positioned where a buck will see them, but scent is another important factor. Some products make mock scrapes more effective and help the attraction last longer.

branch to make it look most natural. Doe-in-heat, buck tarsal or urine scent can be used to get the buck's attention initially. From there, the scent combined with the visual appeal of the scrape is supposed to do the rest.

A MORE SOLID PLAN

Though I've not yet killed a buck in a mock scrape, that doesn't mean I won't continue trying the technique. But today I use it more as a backup plan than my lead plan.

My lead plan is low-profile hunting in high-traffic areas. No scent, no mock scrapes, no fake rubs, no decoy and probably little calling and rattling. I want to see exactly when and where the deer move through my area and let that information later determine if I need to add a component to my setup in order to improve my odds of killing a particular buck. Mock scrapes, like everything else you add to the equation, have as much potential to work against you as for you.

My basis for this belief comes from the years of trapping that my brother, Jeff, and I did trying to earn money for college tuition. Since good raccoon skins were bringing $30 to $40 at the time, we concentrated a lot of our efforts on the masked bandits. Along creeks and marshy shorelines, it was easy to find raccoon tracks and places where they'd form a narrow trail through some kind of natural obstacle. In these places we'd bed a 1½ coil-spring trap, sift dirt over the top to camouflage it and keep everything looking as natural as possible.

These "blind" sets were extremely effective, since the raccoon was simply going about his nightly travels with no indication that anything was out of place. Now we also employed baited sets using fish or strong-smelling raccoon lure scents, and these worked fine too. But there were also times where the bait didn't work. A great blind set was still one of our highest-percentage performers.

I feel the same way about a great stand located in a high-use deer area. The buck might not like the scent you used in the mock scrape, or maybe you inadvertently left some human scent while making the mock scrape. Once you add something that's not entirely natural you alert that buck. He might respond in a positive, aggressive manner and approach. He could also turn tail and run. I've seen it even when I thought I did everything perfectly. I don't like alert deer, I like relaxed deer. But if you need to get their attention to pull them within range, a mock scrape is one tool at your disposal.

The All-Important Licking Branch

Like rubs, some scrapes are referred to as traditional scrapes—meaning that bucks work them from year to year. These traditional scrapes almost always have one constant component: an overhanging licking branch.

Scrapes are made by bucks to communicate with other deer. The bare earth exposed is a visual form of communication, and urination in the scrape is an olfactory form of communication. But many hunters still don't realize the importance of the overhanging branch.

If you've ever watched a buck approach a scrape, his first move is often to sniff the overhanging branch. When bucks work an overhanging branch they deposit scent from their saliva, preorbital glands (near the eyes) and forehead gland. These might be the most important means of identifying that buck to other deer that visit the scrape.

Thus, an overhanging branch is important, whether you're searching for a tradi-

tional scrape or planning to make a mock scrape that looks like the real thing.

The overhanging licking branch is a place for scent communication. Does will also leave their mark at scrapes, to communicate their presence to the local bucks.

WHAT ABOUT RUBS?

ack during my first out-of-state deer hunt in
Missouri, the same hunt I mentioned in the
introduction to this book, I saw buck rubs like
those right out of magazine pictures. So gaudy
they were, so much more impressive than anything I'd ever
seen while hunting near my east-central Wisconsin home,

that I at first doubted their authenticity. I wondered if my
host had rubbed up these trees himself in order to give me
confidence in the area where he'd hung my stand.

But they were real. All it took was one look at the first
couple of bucks to be brought to the meatpole by some of
the other hunters in our camp. These mature, wide-racked

bucks were certainly capable of shredding an 8-inch diameter tree. And ever since that hunt, I've kept my eyes peeled for large rubs. Though not conclusive evidence that an old buck is living in the area, good-sized rubs, and a lot of them, are a good start in selecting your hunting location.

WHY BUCKS RUB

White-tailed bucks can and will rub trees whenever they are in hard-horn. That means that as soon as the velvet is peeled (usually in late August), bucks can begin rubbing trees. Many hunters believe that a good share of rubs that they find are made as the buck attempts to rid its antlers of peeling velvet. However, research indicates that this is not the case. Most rubs appear after the velvet is already gone.

If not to peel velvet, why do bucks rub trees? Rubs serve three purposes.

First and foremost, they are another form of scent communication that identifies a particular buck to the rest of the herd, both bucks and does. When a buck makes a rub, it deposits scent from its forehead and preorbital glands on the tree.

Secondly, a rub is visual. A bright rub against the dark surrounding bark of a tree is a stark visual reminder of a buck's presence in the area. Other deer might first see the rub from a distance and then approach to smell the rub as a way to identify its maker. In fact, extensive research done by Grant Woods revealed that even does will rub their heads on trees previously rubbed by bucks. The importance of scent and visual communication of rubs cannot be overstated.

Finally, bucks rub trees as the rut approaches and their testosterone levels increase. Anxiety and aggression associated with the rut certainly result in a number of rubs as bucks go about their daily travels in anticipation of the rut. Plus, it is thought that the rubbing behavior helps bucks to strengthen neck muscles in preparation for fights with other bucks that might occur in the heat of the rut.

HUNTING RUBS

But are rubs reliable indicators of where a buck will travel? Are they worth you hanging a stand nearby? Most hunters think so; this includes well-known hunter and writer Greg Miller, who's authored multiple books on the topic of rub hunting.

"From the very start of the bow season, as soon as bucks are in hard antler, I'm hunting rub lines," Miller says. "Later on during the rut, I've found that my success rates have gone up when I've concentrated my efforts on rub lines where there is scrape sign also. However, if he's reworking rubs (that aren't near scrapes) I'm going to set up on him. And late in the season, that's where we kill those deer near food sources—on the rub lines. In the big woods where we hunt, the deer use very select corridors. Only a small percentage of that big woods has deer. And rubs are a good indicator

Any tree or bush can feel a buck's wrath. But it seems that bucks prefer to rub certain tree types in certain areas. Learn which tree species your hunting area's bucks like.

Rub lines can reveal a buck's favored travel route. Every rub line, though, is different. Some routes have rubs spread far apart, while others might have rubs every 10 to 20 yards.

because that deer has just showed you where he likes to walk."

Miller often refers to the term "rub line" which basically means multiple rubs spaced from 10 to 50 or more yards apart that show a single buck's preferred travel route. Miller theorizes that by connecting one rub to the next a hunter can diagram how bucks travel about their home range. In areas with good buck-to-doe ratios, this is a reasonable theory, since rubs are generally more prevalent when sex ratios are tighter. But even under these ideal conditions, Miller points out that very few rub lines feature rubs extremely close together, providing an easily followed path through the woods.

"People get into this mentality that they have to find one rub every 10 feet to find a rub line," Miller says. "Every single buck has a different temperature. Some bucks are rub-happy where the rubs might be every 20 yards. But most mature deer don't rub that often. Their meanderings are a lot different than average deer."

"I don't think it's quite as important anymore that you know exactly where a rub line begins and where it ends," Miller continues. "If you find part of it, set up on it."

By "connecting the dots" on a rub line and knowing the lay of the surrounding land, you can often predict where a particular buck is feeding and bedding.

Miller said that once he finds part of a rub line he can generally calculate where the deer is feeding and bedding. He adds that a rub line, in his opinion, is the best location to call from, since it is known to other bucks as a buck travel route.

LOCATING RUBS

This means that good travel corridors are generally those areas where you're going to locate buck rubs. Veteran deer hunter and outdoor writer Charlie Alsheimer looks for funnel areas first, scrapes second and rubs third.

"Rubs equate to a lot in my book, but for me the number one prerequisite is that it's a funnel area and number two that it have scrapes in there and number three that it have rubs," Alsheimer says. "If it has the first two, the rubs are going to be there. Now travel corridors and funnels are more than just a 40-yard-wide patch of woods connecting a larger woods. The edge of where a hardwoods and swamp come together; it could be the top of a ridge that those deer use; it could be a saddle between two mountains; it could be a shallow area in a stream."

North American Hunter field editor Jim Shockey owns and operates a whitetail outfitting business in Saskatchewan. Though he has world-class white-tailed bucks roaming about his territory, he doesn't search out rubs when he's looking for stand sites for his clients. Rubs enter into the equation, but again, they are not the top priority.

"We choose topographically; if the deer are moving through the areas naturally, we set up a stand on it," Shockey says. "If you've chosen your stand site properly, the more deer you have moving through, and you'll have rub lines. I will pick the stand with fresh rubs at it, and we'll know that because of the shavings on the top of the snow. And, in fact, last year the biggest one we killed was killed exactly that way. There was a huge fresh rub when we baited it the day before, so we set the hunter on it that morning."

Thousands of miles away at Mississippi's Tara Wildlife commercial hunting operation, head guide Hank Hearn is also on the lookout for fresh rubs as a means of attempting to pattern bucks for Tara's clients. Hearn said that the rubs are especially important in his strategy before the rut gets going.

"I really put a lot of stock in them, especially early," Hearn says. "Not only does it tell me that there's a buck moving through there, but it gives me his direction of travel and helps me determine that he's going from point A to point B. We have some rubs here that deer rub every year. They're like signpost rubs, and we hunt those quite a bit."

Hearn said that most of these traditional or signpost rubs appear on particular tree types like cypress and sassafras. Some research, like that done by Woods, has indicated that deer prefer to rub certain types of trees and that this preference might be based on the aromatic and/or texture characteristics of the tree. Hearn added that most of the rubs associated with pre-rut behavior begin showing up on Tara's property right around Thanksgiving.

Rubs found along well-worn trails increase the likelihood that a buck will be back through the area. Now the key is settling on a stand location.

BIG RUB, BIG BUCK?

Back to the beginning of this section for a moment. I mentioned the size of some of those rubs that I'd seen in Missouri and the fact that they were the largest I'd ever seen to that point in my deer hunting career. But is it correct to assume that big bucks rub big trees and little bucks, little trees? After all, I did see a couple of very large bucks where I hunted in my youth in Wisconsin, but I never found any of the giant rubs to match.

Hearn says that though he's seen yearling bucks rub their antlers on large-diameter trees, big rubs generally mean big bucks on Tara.

"The height of the rub is really something I look at too," Hearn says in trying to determine how large of a buck made the rub. "Of course, you can also tell the height of his rack in some cases based on the rub."

Shockey agrees with the concept of big rub, big buck, but points out that a big buck might not necessarily make all of his rubs on large-diameter trees.

"One of the biggest bucks I missed was rubbing on a telephone pole and I saw him rubbing it," Shockey says. "So I think there's something to that idea that big bucks rub on big trees, but I think the big bucks will rub on any old thing."

YOU'VE GOT TO BELIEVE

Rubs are certainly an important piece of sign to consider in any whitetail hunting strategy. And that's especially true if you're interested in targeting mature bucks. But how much stock you put in them is up to you. In fact, the real benefit of locating numerous rubs in your hunting area might have more to do with your confidence level on stand and the hours you spend hunting there as opposed to the importance of the rub line itself.

Hearn says that his Tara clients seem happier when they have rubs to look at in the area around their stands. Shockey agrees.

"If I see rubs it makes me focus a little more, keeps me motivated; it's just a reassurance that there are bucks in the area," Shockey says. "So psychologically they are pretty valuable. As far as the reality of a rub helping me get a big buck, I know for a fact that if I would have hunted certain rub lines in the past I'm sure I would have killed that buck. I'm sure that they come back year after year to the same areas and rub the same places; and I think generations of deer do the same things; whatever the habitat reasons. In that sense it also gives me information to work with."

"But most of all, you gotta believe. Or else when that two-second opportunity comes, you're off in Disney World somewhere."

You can tell a lot about a buck by the rub. The size of the tree can be one indicator, but the height of the rub, marks left on surrounding trees and the texture of the rub can also provide information on the headgear the buck is wearing.

DO DECOYS WORK?

Just ask veteran whitetail hunter Greg Miller of Bloomer, Wisconsin. Ask him what it was like to have the biggest typical whitetail of his life approach within bow range as it glared at his decoy.

Miller was hunting in southwestern Iowa as a guest of outfitter Judd Cooney and the Realtree Camouflage video team. A cameraman accompanied Miller to his treestand that day and captured the events for one of Realtree's "Monster Bucks" videotapes.

On that cold morning, Miller rattled up a giant buck that most people who have seen the tape estimate would score something like 190 Boone and Crockett Club points—well above the 170-point minimum and high enough to make it one of the highest-scoring typicals ever taken by a bowhunter. The buck responded aggressively, approaching across an open agricultural field, but Miller says that it was his buck decoy that really did a number on that buck.

"That deer did not just come to my rattling sequence,"

Miller says. "If you watch that deer closely, he's looking at my buck decoy. And that's a world-class deer."

At approximately 20 yards, Miller held a little low to hit the buck in the heart, but the arrow skimmed harmlessly right below the buck. And Miller watched the buck of a lifetime trot off into the Iowa landscape unscathed. Despite the miss, the decoy did its job as it has on a number of other bucks that weren't so fortunate. Miller estimates that decoys are directly responsible for luring nearly a dozen big, mature bucks into range, including a giant 10-point that his brother, Jeff, took in Illinois a few years ago. That buck, Miller says, crossed 200 yards of open winter wheat field to confront the imposter. And, he adds, those dozen or so bucks are probably deer that would never have provided shot opportunities if not for the decoy.

Of course, just like calls and scents, decoys are not 100 percent effective. There are just as many or more times when a buck ignores the decoy. There are even times when a decoy might spook a buck and turn him away from your stand location. But the times when a decoy works make up for it. Once you lure a mature buck close with the aid of a decoy, you'll find yourself hunting over a decoy more often than not.

WHY DECOYS WORK

No matter how much some whitetail hunters will tell you that they have a particular buck buttoned down to a specific trail at a specific time, it just doesn't work that way 99 percent of the time. Oh, sure, early in the season you might have him pegged, but by late September whitetails in most areas are pretty darn unpredictable—at least the mature bucks.

So we choose "high-percentage" spots where we think the odds are good of getting a look at a buck. But there might be a number of different trails that he could take. Will he cross on the ridge or down below? Will he head for those

oaks or the ones right here close to my stand? Whitetails, no matter how hard we try, are hard to pinpoint; especially for bowhunters who need precise stand placement to connect.

So we utilize lures to attract a passing buck that might otherwise stay out of range. We carry rattling horns or grunt calls to appeal to a buck's sense of sound. We use attractant scents of various types in hopes that his acute sense of smell will bring him into range.

The missing link? You've got it. Visual. His eyes. What if he hears a buck grunt or rattling antlers but doesn't see another buck? He gets suspicious, that's what. What if he smells a hot doe or hears a doe bleat but can't see her? Again, suspicion. Sometimes a buck will respond positively to these other stimuli only to stop short because he doesn't get a visual confirmation of what he's expecting. That's where the decoy comes in. That's why it works. Sometimes.

WHERE DECOYS WORK

I've hunted over decoys on a number of occasions when I thought I had the right kind of location to utilize one: relatively open country where deer can see some distance. Both times I've hunted Kansas, for example, I've put a decoy to the test. And though I thought the decoy was in a place where any

Today's decoys are deadly real. More than one whitetail buck has been made a fool by these fakes.

This bedded Feather Flex decoy from Outland Sports is made of foam that makes it collapsible and highly portable. But it must be placed in a wide-open setting in order for a passing deer to spot its low profile.

Never leave an assembled decoy in the woods. Always disassemble the decoy and, if possible, carry it out with you. If you'll be coming back soon and don't want to haul the decoy along, take it apart, bag it and put it in a place where deer won't encounter it.

passing whitetail would spot it, I still haven't had a deer recognize my fakes.

That's a common problem, according to some of the guys who put decoys to work regularly.

"I can't tell you how many times I've set up a decoy in some cover and watched a deer walk right past it without ever seeing it," says well-known deer hunter and photographer Charlie Alsheimer of New York state. "I now place my decoys where deer can readily see them, at the edge of a field or in a well-traveled funnel area."

North American Hunter field editor Jim Shockey, despite hunting in somewhat more broken terrain in Saskatchewan, notices the same problem with whitetails not seeing the decoy.

"Because it's not moving, it doesn't necessarily catch his eye as he's moving through there," Shockey says, "I do use a decoy every single time I can carry them in there and I've never seen it be a negative factor; it's been a neutral factor many times, nine times out of 10, but one time out of 10 it's a positive factor and at that point I'm net ahead. The only problem is the practicality of moving them around. They're heavy and awkward and noisy, and the lighter ones just aren't real enough for where I hunt anyway."

USING DECOYS

Despite the not-so-portable nature of many deer decoys, never leave a decoy out in your hunting area while you are not hunting. Of course, it could be stolen, but more importantly, you don't want to give the deer an opportunity to discover it while you're not there. Decoys capture the curiosity of a passing deer, but a decoy might only work one time on a particular animal. If a buck, or doe for that matter, has an opportunity to investigate a decoy and finally spooks after realizing it's a fake, your odds of bringing that deer to a decoy again are dramatically diminished.

So don't leave your decoy sitting out in your hunting area when you're not there, not even for an hour. Miller says that on private property he and his hunting partners often disassemble their decoys and hide them in an area where the deer won't encounter them. That way, the hunters don't have to carry the decoy in and out of the woods every time they use one.

It's also critical to anchor your decoy securely so that it's not blown over by the wind nor easily knocked over by a frisky buck. Of course, a flat area makes this job easier and so does soft soil where you can press the legs of the decoy into the earth an inch or two.

WHEN DECOYS WORK

Decoys are especially effective during the weeks surrounding the rut. Bucks are aggressively seeking out does, they've mixed it up with other bucks to establish dominance, and they're interested in any other deer that they encounter.

Earlier in this decoy piece, I referred to the fact that I've put decoys to the test on a couple of Kansas bowhunts during the rut. On the first hunt with my friends from Lohman Game Calls, the Flambeau Redi-Doe decoy looked great to me, but I never had it positioned just right to capture a buck's attention.

A couple of years later I was a guest of North American Hunting Club Members Sam and Frieda Lancaster who own beautiful Claythorne Lodge in southeastern Kansas. Sam and Frieda are both avid bowhunters and Sam had a Flambeau decoy there that he had "souped up" with a servo motor and remote control moveable tail. Sam encouraged me to try the decoy early on in my bowhunt, but I chose my usual low-profile approach and ended up regretting it on the second-to-last day of the hunt.

About 8 a.m. I spotted a nice 2½-year-old, 8-point buck chasing a doe about 100 yards behind my stand. In hopes of grabbing his attention, I raked my hand aggressively across my Lohman rattle box. I lost sight of the buck for a few moments and assumed that he had kept going after the doe, but moments later he appeared marching stiff-legged toward my tree, hair bristling on his back and neck. He stopped at about 75 yards, so I tried to urge him to keep coming with my grunt call. It worked! Each step got my heart pumping faster, 70 yards, 65, 60 ... 50. Then the buck put on the brakes again.

I was a good 25 feet up in a large oak at the point of a narrow brushline separating two open, grassy fields. The buck stood his ground and glared as he searched for the source of the buck sounds I'd thrown out. Not seeing another deer in the open terrain, he turned and headed back in the direction where the doe had disappeared. Twice more I rattled and grunted that buck back to the exact same 50-yard spot, but he would not come another step closer. If ever there was a time I needed a decoy, this was it! And that's how it goes with a decoy—when you need one, you really need it! The next day I had the doe ready and waiting, but, of course, no mature bucks showed.

Hunter's Specialties promotional coordinator Steve Puppe believes that decoys could be effective outside of the rut, too.

"You could probably use decoys right at the start of the season in September," Puppe says. "At that time I would probably use it as a buck since the bucks are in bachelor groups."

Puppe bow-killed two mature bucks last season, one in Kansas and one in Iowa, while hunting over a decoy. Both were rut

hunts, but the timing of the rut determined his decoy strategy.

"Ninety percent of the time, I use a buck decoy," Puppe says. "You want to use it as a buck before they're actually breeding. Then when it comes into that breeding time, I would use it as a doe."

IF YOU GO WITH A DOE

Positioning a decoy can mean the difference between success and failure. Not just where you set it, but exactly how it is positioned can make all the difference in the world when

Decoy positioning requires attention to detail. Bucks will often approach a doe decoy from behind, so the decoy should be placed quartering away from the stand at about 20 to 25 yards. Buck decoys, on the other hand, should be quartering toward the stand at about 20 yards because bucks will confront other bucks head-on.

you consider that shot angles and distance (especially for you bowhunters) will come into play.

DISTANCE

Let's start with distance. Obviously, the closer you place a decoy to your stand, the more risk you take of being seen. Some hunters trust that the decoy will have the buck's full attention, so they don't worry about keeping the decoy close. Other hunters feel more comfortable allowing more room to the decoy. Alsheimer says that he chooses a doe decoy about 75 percent of the time when he's hunting during some phase of the rut.

"I like to locate the decoy 20 to 25 yards upwind of my stand, with the decoy quartering away," Alsheimer says. "In the majority of cases, a buck will circle a doe decoy rather than come straight to it. Second, if a buck suspects something is odd about the scene, it will hang up within 20 to 30 yards behind the decoy. If that happens, you're still able to get a shot and probably at point-blank range."

Wind

From there it's a matter of wind, and angle. Of course, you want the decoy upwind or crosswind of your stand position. The last thing you want is for the decoy to work perfectly, right up until the time when the buck is only steps away

As always, scent control is important; bucks will likely circle downwind of the decoy if they are at all suspicious about the setup.

from it and catches your human scent.

You can't control the very real possibility of the buck circling downwind after spotting your decoy. A mature buck is apt to take this precaution whenever he's skeptical. This is a risk you take whenever you use a call or a decoy to bring deer to you. And it's also why human scent control is so critically important. (See Chapter 1 for more information.)

Angle

Angle matters too. A buck will most often stop behind a doe decoy at some point. He might approach head-on, but he'll probably eventually circle and approach from the rear if he's genuinely interested. Imagine him single file at the same

angle a few feet behind your doe decoy. If, from your stand that gives you a broadside or slightly quartering-away angle and a clear shooting lane, you're all set.

GETTING BUCKY

Now, you would think that during the rut a buck would be more likely to approach a doe decoy than a buck; but that's not what Miller has found.

"I always use a buck," Miller says. "The buck decoy basically eliminates attracting antlerless deer. Guys say, well why wouldn't you want to attract the does during the rut if the bucks are going to be with them? But if I get a bunch of does curious about my doe decoy, eventually one of them figures out something is wrong.

"Buck decoys, however, attract hot does, plain and simple. I've had three occasions where a hot doe was being tended and came running to my buck decoy, and you can imagine what that tending buck was thinking about that. There is no doubt in my mind that if you have a doe decoy in a lot of situations, he's not going to pay it any attention."

Miller's reasoning is a lot like that of many turkey hunters who have caught on to the effectiveness of the jake decoy. Gobblers will often respond more aggressively to these young male intruders and approach in an attempt to run off the competition.

Rack size is an important consideration. Some decoys are offered with an optional rack kit, but some hunters choose to fashion their own set of antlers for use on a decoy.

Alsheimer thinks that antler size makes a big difference in the effectiveness of a buck decoy. He says that antlers should represent those bucks from the area being hunted. Where good numbers of mature bucks are present, he might attach antlers that would score in the 125-inch class. In areas with fewer mature bucks, a 100-inch set of antlers might be better.

As far as positioning goes, the decoy should again be upwind, of course, but this time you should assume that the buck will confront the buck decoy head-on. Thus, a perfectly broadside or slightly quartering-to angle on the decoy would be best.

Here the distance is up to you, but the closer you get to your stand the higher the odds that the buck will be alerted to your presence. If you're bowhunting and have a good opening at a comfortable range of 20 or 30 yards, that's a good place for the decoy. Again, gun hunters don't have to be quite as concerned with the distance and might well opt to keep the decoy 100 yards or so from the stand to avoid detection by an approaching deer. Anticipate the shot angle, though, when the deer approaches and stops to confront the decoy.

WHAT SMELLS?

Scent use in conjunction with decoys is another area where hunters have difficulty agreeing. Some argue that a

Decoys can do the job visually, but if they contain human odors, they'll fail you. Be careful about keeping decoys free of foreign smells that can alert whitetails.

Adding attractant scents like buck urine, tarsal scent or doe-in-heat can hold a buck's interest in the decoy longer. Some hunters choose to go scent-free with decoys, others like the added attraction of deer lure.

decoy is visual and, thus, doesn't require to be juiced up with any scent. Others say that scent applied to a decoy can keep an interested buck in the area longer.

Probably most important is to concentrate on keeping your decoy free of any human odor, and other foreign odors for that matter. Storing a decoy in a garage where there are a variety of odors from gas, cleaning solutions and pets can cause you trouble when you try to hunt over that smelly decoy. And when a deer reacts negatively to the decoy, you might end up blaming the decoy itself if you didn't know the truth—the deer smelled you or something else it didn't like coming from the decoy.

Just as you would use scent destroyers on your outer clothing and other hunting equipment, consider dousing your decoy with the same from time to time. And store it in a sealed container to protect it from coming in contact with other odors. From there, what about trying the perfect cover scent—deer droppings? What could be more natural than that?

Miller says that he likes to use a dominant buck urine scent in conjunction with his decoy, but that he sprays it on the ground near the decoy, not on the decoy. That way he doesn't have to worry about the scent attracting a deer to his

decoy when he's hid it between hunts. He said that he learned the hard way when he applied scent directly to a decoy, took it down, hid it and came back later in the day to find the decoy pushed out of the cover and into a nearby field. He doesn't know how big the buck was that did it, but it was a deer all right; probably one that would be a lot harder to fool the second time around.

MOVING PARTS?

Movement on a deer decoy is a point of contention, even among veteran deer hunters who have spent time hunting over decoys and witnessing deer behavior toward decoys.

Alsheimer prefers to have the option to cause some movement on the decoy to keep a deer's attention. In the past he has tied a white handkerchief to the deer's rump and attached a length of fishing line to be able to make it move.

Lancaster's doe decoy mentioned earlier in this section was souped up with a servo motor (like those used on remote controlled cars or airplanes) mounted on the inside back of the decoy near the rump. Lancaster then used model airplane linkage material to connect the servo motor to a real deer tail that he attached to the decoy. With joystick remote

control in hand, he can operate the tail from up to 75 yards away, moving the tail in any direction and at whatever speed he chooses with the joystick.

"I had several deer look at the plain decoy from a distance and not come in," Lancaster says. "It gave me the idea that if it moved it would attract more deer. I believe it works."

Puppe says that he agrees with Lancaster that when used as a doe, a decoy is more effective with a little bit of movement.

"When I use it as a buck I want it still," Puppe says. "But if I use it as a doe I'll attach a little tissue on the tail for movement. That way I can spray a little bit of doe-in-heat scent right on the tissue and not have any scent on the decoy itself."

Don't put deer lure directly on the decoy. You're better off putting it on the ground near the decoy or on an applicator attached to the decoy. That way you can change your approach day-to-day with an odor-free decoy.

Decoy Notes

SAFETY

No matter when or where you utilize a deer decoy, safety must be a consideration. Not the safety of the decoy, but *your* safety.

Using a decoy during the general firearms seasons in most places is too dangerous to consider. The decoys on the market today are so lifelike that they can fool an excited hunter, especially if the decoy wears antlers.

Whenever you're transporting a decoy, even during bow season, it's wise to hang some orange flagging off it. Or, better yet, disassemble the decoy and carry it in a large duffle bag. Some decoys, like the foam Sport Flex models from Outland Sports, have blaze orange on parts of the decoy to make it more visible to surrounding hunters, thereby increasing safety.

SOURCES

Here are some of the various deer decoys on the market. For more information on the features of particular models shown here, contact the manufacturers listed.

Carry-Lite Decoys, Dept. NAH,
5203 W. Clinton Ave. Milwaukee, WI 53223.
(Visit your local sporting goods retailer.)

Come-Alive Decoy Products, Dept. NAH,
4916 Seton Pl., Greendale, WI 53129.

Flambeau Products Corp., Dept. NAH,
1581 Valplast Rd. Middlefield, OH 44062.

Mel Dutton Decoys, Dept. NAH,
Box 113, Faith, SD 57626.

Outland Sports, Feather Flex Decoys, Dept. NAH,
4500 Doniphan Drive, Box 220, Neosho, MO 64850.

CALLING & RATTLING

espite how much we've learned about white-tailed deer and deer hunting, calling whitetails still results in confusion and doubt among hunters. Calling deer is not difficult and it can be incredibly effective. Of course, the deer still have three ways that they can respond to a vocalization or the sound of rattling antlers: positively, negatively or neutrally. One old football coach used to say about passing the ball that, "three things can happen and two of them are bad."

But whitetail hunting is for the moment, and at some moments a call can make your season.

SOUNDS DEER MAKE: GRUNTS

If you've hunted whitetails for a few years and have had the opportunity to hunt outside of the regular firearms season, you've probably heard one or more forms of whitetail vocalization. For hunters, the most intriguing is the buck grunt. We'll not get into the various types of grunts that researchers have tried to isolate and define. For our purposes a buck grunt is a buck grunt because it's almost impossible for the hunter to know what type of grunt a buck is going to respond to at any given time. And unlike a turkey or duck call, there's no art to blowing a deer grunt call.

"Deer calling and grunting, in particular, is the easiest form of calling," says Lohman Game Calls' Brad Harris. "I believe that most of the things people hear (about how to blow a grunt call) is hogwash. If a deer hears a grunt and he's in the right mood, he's going to come to it."

Bucks grunt for a variety of reasons. Sometimes it's an attempt to intimidate another buck during the rut. Sometimes a buck grunts when he's chasing or tending a doe. And other times bucks will be walking through the woods alone and grunting every few steps for no apparent reason whatsoever. Maybe they're old and senile and talking to themselves! Generally buck grunts are short notes less than a second long. Sometimes they are separated by long pauses, other times they are more staccato and rapid in nature, like when a buck is chasing a doe through the woods.

Lohman's Brad Harris rattled in this fine buck with the aid of the Lohman rattle box. Harris and other veteran hunters call often—and not just during the rut. As Harris points out, bucks begin sparring as soon as antler velvet peels.

"Deer grunt year-round, and I have video while turkey hunting of bucks walking through the woods grunting; and that's when their antlers are just starting to poke through their head," Harris says. "You can grunt deer up anytime. Contact grunts are a natural vocal sound that deer utilize year-round. Anytime a deer is active and moving and he hears a grunt, you have a chance of him coming to investigate it."

Mark Drury demonstrates the M.A.D.D. Grunt-Snort-Wheeze call that can really get a rutting buck cranked up. Drury says that about 70 percent of the bucks on their videos are called in front of the camera.

OTHER SOUNDS: BLEATS & SNORTS

Does also grunt from time to time, but it is more common to hear does and fawns make a bleat call. A bleat can be a soft call that sounds kind of like a young calf. Soft bleats seem to simply be a means of deer letting one another know where they are or to call family groups together. Loud bleats, on the other hand, can be produced by both does and fawns and are usually distress calls.

Of course, all deer hunters have heard the "snort" produced by a whitetail when it catches our human scent. This is a call that won't attract deer, but at least one call manufac-

turer has a call on the market to produce the snort as a means of stopping a running deer in order to get a shot. This might be effective for rifle hunters in some situations.

Bucks also make a call called the snort-wheeze which is an aggressive call most often heard right before or after a fight. Bucks use this call in an attempt to ward off another buck. Like rattling, it can lure in deer, but it is a difficult sound to reproduce.

GRUNT CALLS

On the other hand, everybody has a grunt call, despite the fact that this is a relatively easy sound to reproduce. It sounds something like a pig, and if you've heard enough buck grunts, you can probably replicate it pretty well without a call. *North American Hunter* field editor Jim Shockey grunts at bucks without the aid of a manufactured call. Still, for volume control and a more exact replication of the sound, a manufactured call is a good idea. Besides, most of them are very inexpensive.

In fact, volume control might be the most important consideration when you're trying to grunt a white-tailed buck into range.

"I believe that volume is the biggest factor in calling a deer," Harris says. "Some guys said that if you could hear a grunt call past 50 yards you were blowing it too loudly. That's not true. You have to have the common sense to call to the conditions. If the deer is a long way off or if it's windy, you have to increase the volume. Volume is the key. Keep the grunts to semi-short contact grunts."

Brad's words remind me of an Iowa bowhunt not too long ago. During the five-day bowhunt I'd seen one good record-class buck on three different occasions. One still morning I blew my grunt call as he walked by at approximately 70 yards. The buck never raised an ear and kept on walking. I hit the grunt call again. Nothing. The third time I hit it with a little more force, and that stopped him and turned an ear in my direction. He paused for about five seconds and went on walking toward three does a short distance ahead.

The last day of the hunt, it was a windy and raw mid-November day. Midmorning I spotted a buck moving at a fast walk across a brushy pasture about 100 yards from my stand. I hit the grunt call, and the deer never broke stride. Too soft. I doubled the force on the next note, and the buck made a hairpin turn and stiff-legged it right for my tree with his hair standing on end. The 2½-year-old buck was an aggressive one that apparently wasn't afraid to mix it up. I arrowed him at 25 yards, but surely never would have had the chance if not for cranking up the volume on my grunt call.

The tone of your grunts can also make a difference, according to Harris.

"The only other thing is that I don't believe in the real deep grunt calls; the higher tonality calls seem best," Harris says. "But other than that, there's no doing it wrong. If you grunt and he hears you, it's all up to the deer."

WHAT ABOUT THE BLEAT?

Most hunters think only of the buck grunt when they are attempting to harvest a deer, but even if you're after a buck exclusively, doe and fawn bleats can work. The key, according to Harris, is in what you say.

"Again, I just use a contact bleat," Harris says. "It's non-distressful, all you're saying is, 'I'm a deer, come over here.' Deer are social animals; they like to be around other deer. As the rut progresses, a doe bleat followed by a grunt or two is like using two turkey calls. It's like a jake yelp and then yelping like a hen. It works extremely well."

Harris doesn't like distressful, loud adult deer bleats. But fawn distress calls have proven effective in attracting adult does—often on the run! So, if you have an antlerless tag, a fawn bleat can be a very important whitetail vocalization to consider.

Grunt calls don't carry as far as rattling, but they can be the ticket to coaxing a buck those final few steps into range. Don't worry about producing the perfect grunt; the deer's mood will determine his response.

RATTLE & ROLL

Imitating the sounds of two bucks fighting, or "rattling," has become a technique that some hunters have embraced and others have virtually ignored. The fact, however, that most of the people in the business of producing deer hunting videos (people who make a good portion of their living by successfully harvesting mature whitetailed bucks) rely on rattling is testament to its effectiveness. And all you have to do is look at the results to realize that it can and does work.

Mark Drury, founder of M.A.D.D. Game Calls, is one of those hunters who never goes to the whitetail

Battling bucks often draw a crowd of onlookers. Both bucks and does may respond to the sound of a fight. In areas with a good buck-to-doe ratio and buck age structure, rattling works all the better.

woods without his rattling antlers or rattle box. And can you blame him? In October, 1998, Mark called in and killed the biggest buck of his life while hunting in Illinois.

"It was warm early in the day and then a cold front came in and the wind blew out of the northwest," Mark says. "My brother, Terry, had set up a stand for a northwest wind with a big brushpile on the downwind side of the stand.

"I rattled at about 4:30 p.m., just some light sparring. At about 5 p.m. Terry said, 'Okay, you woke him up, now let him hear you.' We have a new grunt-snort-wheeze call. I

grunted a couple of times and then did a couple of snort-wheeze calls to make it sound like two bucks coming together. Then I banged the antlers together really heavily, and it just rang through that bottom. I did that for about 45 seconds, and he showed up maybe five minutes later."

He was a big, old non-typical that approached to 20 yards and froze for two or three minutes, Drury says, looking for the fight. The buck made a scrape and hit an overhanging branch as it postured for the bucks that it thought were nearby. Finally, he moved in even closer, pausing at five yards but still quartering to Drury. When the buck turned to head back in the direction he came, however, Drury took the quartering-away opportunity and made it count. The buck ended up scoring 184⅞ net non-typical, a giant in anyone's book.

"Most of the deer we kill on the videos come to calling, probably 60 or 70 percent," Drury says. "We have confidence in it and we do it all the time. When that buck gets to be 4 or 5 years old, he gets lazy and doesn't move much during daylight hours. So if they're not up and freely moving, you gotta give them a reason to get up and move.

"You're painting an audio picture out there," Drury continues. "The more natural you can make it, the more realistic, you'll elicit more response."

When it comes to gear, Drury says he usually chooses the grunt call as his first weapon on an out-of-range buck. If that doesn't pull him

Mark Drury, left, rattled in his best buck ever in Illinois while his brother, Terry, captured the events on videotape. This is one of those old bucks that the Drury's might never have seen if not for having the confidence to call.

Whether you choose real antlers or a rattling device for your calling, you have to decide how aggressive you want your calling to be. That often depends on the time of the season. Loud, aggressive rattling is often best just before and after the peak of the rut.

toward his stand, Drury goes for the rattling antlers or rattle box. He says that he likes real antlers for volume but that the Lohman rattle box and the M.A.D.D. Power Rattle provide the tools to call with less movement. When a buck's in view but still out of range, Drury says he'll simply do some light one-handed calling with the Power Rattle at his side and that this can be the ticket for making the buck commit the rest of the way.

Like all hunters, though, Drury says that he has many bucks circle downwind, some of which eventually spook after picking up his human scent. The exception, he says, are the dominant bucks that know they are the dominant buck in the woods. These animals, Drury says, will sometimes boldly head directly for the source of the fight.

Still, he says, stand placement is critical and Drury now looks for calling locations that include some kind of downwind obstacle or land structure that will turn a buck to his stand before it gets downwind. Maybe it's a creek, bluff or fenceline. Even a large brushpile like the one incorporated into that Illinois setup. But planning for a buck's approach in response to a call can help you achieve a happy ending to the hunt.

A happy ending to one memorable Saskatchewan hunt turned Jim Shockey into a proponent of rattling.

"It wasn't successful for me for one main reason; I didn't use them (rattling antlers) religiously," Shockey says. "Then one day it was my only option. I could see the buck too far away for my muzzleloader and clanked on them, and he turned on a dime. I literally shot him running straight at me at 20 yards. And from that point on I realized, 'Hey, these do work.' If you use them in the right situation with the right buck, he will come in."

RATTLING THE RIGHT WAY

Like grunt calls, rattling doesn't have to be confined to the rut. As Harris points out, bucks will spar and fight any time after the velvet has peeled.

"I do use it early in the season when the bucks are sparring," Harris says. "There are more antlers touching at that time of the year than any other, but it's a different, non-aggressive sound. Just like a little push-and-shove match as they're gearing up for the real thing. I do rattle throughout the deer season. I just don't do it as aggressively outside of the rut."

A lot of hunters are unsure about how often they should rattle and how long a typical rattling sequence should last.

Two hunters can team up to rattle bucks in close. In this way, the hunter is always at the ready with hands on bow or gun and eyes fixed on the surrounding cover.

There are no hard and fast rules here, but there are some guidelines for rattling technique.

"I'll rattle as often as every 20 or 30 minutes, or maybe just once an hour," Harris says. "It kind of depends on what kind of mood I'm in. A typical sequence is about 12 to 15 seconds of rattling, a pause, a few grunts; then repeat that twice more. Then I might not rattle again for an hour. It's kind of like trolling. If you drag that bait around long enough, something's going to bite it."

YOU DON'T NEED PERFECTION

To prove, though, how imprecise rattling technique is, Hunter's Specialties' Steve Puppe recalls a buck he rattled up when he wasn't even trying.

"I was carrying in a deer stand and using a ladder that had these little nylon straps with belt buckle things and they were banging on the steel and that was enough to call him in," Puppe says, remembering the curious buck that came in for a look. "So I don't think that the tone is as critical as some people think."

Puppe's point is well-taken. A lot of deer hunters think that many deer hunting techniques have to be just so in order to work. In reality, no two hunters rattle exactly the same or blow a grunt call exactly the same. The reason that so many different-sounding grunt calls or rattling sequences work is that every white-tailed buck is an individual. And there's really no way to know, until you try, exactly what call is going to turn him on.

The bottom line, as Drury and the rest of the veteran deer hunters in this article point out, is to call with confidence. It will not work a lot more times than it will, but don't be discouraged. The experts bat a low percentage on calling too. But when it does work, you'll be hooked on calling up whitetails. And this experience will, ultimately, help you hunt whitetails successfully.

Can Deer Become Call-Shy?

Though whitetails don't usually hear as much artificial calling as say a wild turkey, duck or goose, most veteran deer callers agree that deer can become call-shy in extreme situations.

While bowhunting at Willow Point in Mississippi a few years ago, I remember talking to a couple of the guides who warned against calling in most situations. Though Willow Point has an exceptional deer herd and a well-managed buck-to-doe ratio, hunting pressure is an issue. And after years of a lot of those hunters tooting on grunt calls and clashing rattling antlers, bucks on Willow Point seem to shy from the calling in a lot of cases.

Even where deer are lightly hunted, a whitetail that smells human scent after initially coming to

Like turkeys or waterfowl, bucks that have had a bad experience after coming to a call (detecting human odor or dodging a bullet or arrow) are more difficult to call in a second time. On heavily hunted public land, hunters must consider the issue of call-shyness.

a call will be more difficult to call close a second time. And that means that if you're banking on one particular buck, you must pay close attention to the stand setup and the wind before you roll the dice on calling. Because if he busts you before you can get a good shot, odds are fair that he won't come to a call again that season.

In most areas, whitetails are not over-called. In fact, the private or public property that you deer hunt has probably seen very little attempt at calling whitetails. Thus, your odds of success are increased, provided that the herd is relatively well-managed with a decent buck-to-doe ratio and some mature bucks in the herd. But deer on some commercial hunting operations hear a lot more calling from hunters.

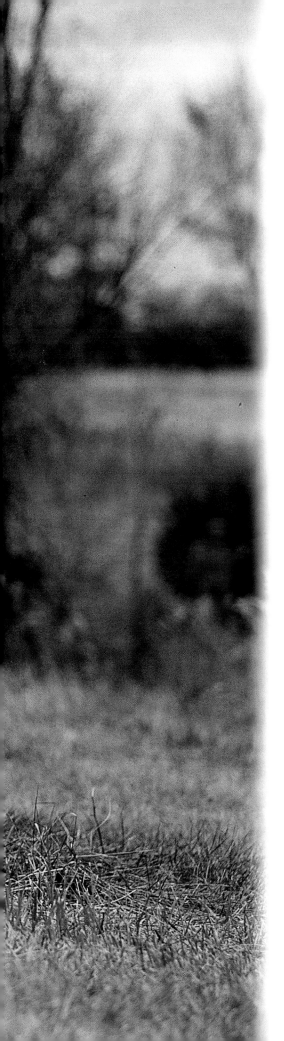

Chapter 4

SOLID TACTICS

Getting a look at an undisturbed, in-range whitetail that is offering a good shot angle is, of course, the goal for anyone reading this book. There are a number of ways to get there. Each has its merits and its particular challenges. And each will be discussed in this chapter.

You can, as the vast majority of deer hunters do, take a stand and wait for deer to naturally travel within range of your position. Or, while on stand, you can attempt to call or lure deer to you with a variety of methods. Whitetails taken by stand hunters comprise the vast majority of the deer harvest across the country.

But if you're after a little more challenge or live in an area where deer densities are relatively low, you can try to hone your foot-hunting skills. Stalking, still-hunting and tracking all put you at eye level, where movement and scent are much more easily detected by radar-equipped whitetails. Yet, there is a time and place for every one of these hunting methods.

Hunting whitetails successfully is often about playing the hand that you are dealt. If you go to the deer woods always a stand hunter never willing to try something a little different, you are going to handicap yourself from time to time. And you are going to miss out on the valuable lesson of being versatile. What do you do when the bass aren't hitting top-water stuff? You try something else until you find what works. The same flexibility is important for deer hunters.

Come along and we'll show you.

TAKING A STAND

aybe you fancy yourself a still-hunter or a tracker. You say you like to make things happen rather than wait for deer that might or might not pass within view of your stand. This certainly is your prerogative, and topic for conversation a few pages further into this book, but it will probably mean that you'll kill less deer.

Whoa! Wait a second! Some guy from Maine just slammed the book shut and is looking for an address where he can write an angry letter to this stand hunter from Wisconsin. In the forests of Maine, after all, where deer densities are low and the forest density high, all a deer stand might produce in

a week of hunting is a good case of claustrophobia. Same holds true in the eastern provinces of Canada. Okay, I'll admit it. A very few of you might be better served at times to hunt afoot. But the vast majority of deer hunters and prospective deer hunters reading this book understand the value of a perfectly positioned deer stand.

WHY STANDS WORK

Stand hunting for whitetails makes sense; and with no statistics available to back me up on this one, I'll venture to guess that at least 95 percent of the white-tails killed across North America each year are killed by hunters sitting or standing in one place waiting for a deer to appear. Wolves are good on their feet; we human hunters are rather pathetic on the move against a wild creature as tuned as a white-tailed deer.

Know that you put yourself at a disadvantage when you start to move about the woods. Our human eyes are exceptional when it comes to perceiving detail and color, but we don't spot movement nearly as well as whitetails. So, who's going to see whom first in this game?

Then there's sound. Most still-hunters and trackers, like my friend from Maine, who I hope is still with me, pick their days to hunt afoot. They wait for a pow-dery blanket of snow or a soaking rain to muffle their footfalls. If that kind of a day also brings a stiff wind of 15 or 20 miles per hour or more, all the better to camouflage the hunter's movement with whipping tree branches. Wind also oblit-erates the noise of a boot snapping a twig or rolling a small rock. And a steady, stiff wind is not as fickle about changing its course during the final sneak to get an open shot. But even on those rare days when all these elements come together, the whitetails still somehow seem to know we're near.

Now think of the advantages of a deer stand. Every minute we spend in a stand we are (or should be if we've done our home-work) in an area with a high probability of deer traffic. Things like trails, feeding areas and funnels mean that deer will likely show within view of our stand if we put in our time. Conversely, the tracker or still-hunter is not always in a prime location to see deer. If we sit still as we should on a deer stand, odds are good that we see the deer before it sees us. And this, I'm convinced, is a most critical factor in hunting whitetails successfully.

Feeding areas are a natural place for stand hunters to concentrate their efforts. Whether it's an oak ridge or a food plot, as long as there is fresh deer sign, the whitetails are sure to show up sooner or later.

It sounds obvious. But many deer hunters fail in sitting still and see more white tails waving goodbye than they do deer in a riflescope. Furthermore, white-tailed deer, maybe more than any other big game animal in North America, are predictable. At least they're predictable enough and live most of their lives on small enough home ranges so that a stand placed in the right tree or brush pile should give us a look at most of the deer in the area.

As I said earlier, I'm probably not telling most of you anything new when it comes to espousing the merits of stand hunting. So let's get into the nuts and bolts of how to hunt better from the stands we choose.

TREESTANDS: A CASE STUDY

In some respects, treestands deserve something more like an entire chapter rather than part of a single section. After all, they are the downfall of most whitetails these days. They get us above the deer's line of sight and at least slightly improve the chances that our human odor will waft over the head of a nearby whitetail. That, at least, is how it is supposed to work. But whitetails in many areas have learned to look for us hunters lurking in trees.

For the past couple of seasons, I've finished my deer hunting travels on Louisiana's Willow Point Island in the Mississippi River. The 6,500-acre island is part of the Tara Wildlife commercial hunting operation located near Vicksburg, Mississippi. The season opens October 1 and doesn't close until late in January, and during that time approximately 140 bowhunters come to the island to hunt. Meanwhile, the 1,200 or so deer on that island try to keep tabs on where the stands are and which ones are inhabited by humans. Willow Point's head guide, Tom Jones, is charged with the monumental task of trying to stay one step ahead of the deer. And he's come up with some creative treestand techniques to improve the odds of his clients killing a mature buck. In fact, despite the intense hunting pressure, Willow Point Island churns out an average of 15 Pope and Young

Head guide Hank Hearn (center) of Tara Wildlife in Mississippi talks hunting stategy with some of his clients after a morning bowhunt. The guides at Tara have come up with creative ways to put treestand hunters within range of hunt-wise whitetails.

Club record-book bucks each season. These are all strategies and ideas you could put to use where you hunt, albeit on a smaller scale!

Jones and his guides pull all the 200 portable, hang-on stands at the end of each hunting season. Weeks before the season begins in October, they're back out hanging up to 45 of the fixed-position stands at the top of sectional ladders. The stands start lower (15 to 18 feet) early in the season only because the foliage is so thick in the Southeast at this time of the year. A lower stand is the only way to find any shooting lanes to the deer below. Whereas most of us hang our stands facing in the direction that we expect the deer to come from, Jones often does the opposite. His reasoning here is that he wants to utilize the tree trunk to help hide the hunter as the deer approach. In fact, one of his long-time guides, Kirby McGuffie, says that when a deer is heading toward his tree, he'll press himself close to the trunk and try to hide his face from view. These deer are born in the shadows of treestands. Most of them have seen a hunter in a tree, been shot at, or seen another deer shot or shot at by a treestand hunter. To arrow a totally unsuspecting deer on this island is quite a feat.

Once the woods start opening up toward the end of November, the fixed-position stands go higher in the trees; 30 feet is not out of the question. And throughout the season more stands are being hung so that Jones and the other guides can rest areas and move hunters every day as the wind and deer movements warrant. By mid-season all 200 of the hang-on stands will be in use and 120 to 125 trees for climbing stands will be marked. Jones keeps a detailed record of where the various stands are. Surrounding cover to break the human outline is a luxury not often found in these trees, so Jones and the other guides do very little trimming around the stands. The guides are confident of where the shot will come if it comes at all, so they make sure that there's an opening to that spot, but that's about it. In addition to the fixed-position stands, Jones sometimes sends hunters out with one of the many climbing stands also in his arsenal. When a good buck is spotted in an area where there isn't a stand, or if Jones doesn't want to risk bumping the buck by

The author with an 8-point buck taken on Willow Point Island in Mississippi. Despite a 25-foot-high tree-stand and good wind direction, this buck spotted the setup just as the arrow was released. It was too late for him, but it's testament to how whitetails are learning to look up.

going in to hang a stand, he'll send the hunter in with a stand and ready to hunt. That way, the first time the deer notices something's not quite right, it's too late.

OTHER TREESTAND TACTICS

Jones utilizes some additional treestand tactics that are important to consider.

"A lot of times that deer knows where the stand is," Jones says. "If I know that he knows where it's at, I'll leave that stand in the tree and put another one up (nearby). Sometimes I'll have three empty stands up in three different trees and a hunter in a fourth."

Jones believes that once a deer determines where a stand is, it might not drastically alter its travel route but rather skirt the stand at 60 or so yards, just out of bow range. When that starts happening, Jones starts adding stands to the equation until he outguesses the deer.

Recently I took an 8-point buck on Willow Point. Jones had set the stand a couple of days before my arrival and no one had hunted it. I waited there a solid 25 feet off the ground with a cameraman in a stand a couple feet above me, hoping that the deer would filter out of the swamp and toward the food plot behind us. The 8-point came in perfectly along the upwind trail where Jones said he would. At 20 yards, and just before he cleared one last thick-trunked tree, I

Moving stand locations is critical to success. Even excellent funnel areas can be over-hunted, causing deer to change their travel routes. If you go for two or three sits without seeing the deer you're looking for, it might be time to find a new tree.

drew my bow. The buck paused behind a small sapling, stepped clear, and looked up at me just as I touched the trigger of my release. He ducked, but it was too late as the arrow drove deep into his chest. I don't know what that deer heard or saw, maybe we were somewhat silhouetted against the late afternoon sky, but I doubt that there are many places in North America where a whitetail can spot a treestand like on Willow Point. Thanks to Tom's approach to stand placement, though, I notched my tag on a nice Southeastern whitetail and ended my season on a high note.

Admittedly, the Willow Point scenario is extreme. But I think most eastern, southern and midwestern whitetail hunters will agree that deer aren't as ignorant about treestands as they used to be. Take a chunk of public land in states like Pennsylvania, Ohio or Wisconsin and try to get away with a shabby treestand setup. It ain't going to work. These deer have been there, done that.

On the other side of the coin, I spent five days in Montana on a September whitetail hunt and saw something like 100 whitetails and never had one really pin me down in the stand. That's why I'm going back out there again; I like my odds for success on deer that haven't yet wised up quite as much as their Eastern counterparts.

EXPLORING THE HIGH ROAD

You've probably read it in other places in this book, but it bears repeating. I like high stands for most of my whitetail hunting. I might not go quite as high on average as the Willow Point guys, but 18 to 20 feet is about as low as I want to go. I've just had better success at these heights, and most of my friends who deer hunt a lot from treestands agree with that opinion. Now, again, if you don't feel comfortable up this high, by all means hunt lower. Deer hunting is supposed to be fun, and you won't have fun if you're worried about your stand's height. And no matter how high you hunt, wear a safety harness.

Some deer hunters argue that shot angles from these high stands are more difficult, especially for the bowhunter. I haven't found this to be true. A deer's vital chest cavity is about the same in width and depth. So even if I'm shooting more down on a deer, I have a target area that is just as large as if I were on the ground. I do have the spine to contend with, and would rather not hit a deer in the spine, but if I do, I'm confident that my arrow will have enough energy to kill the deer instantly, especially at close range right under a tree.

If I miss the spine as intended, the arrow will likely pass completely through, exiting very low behind the front legs, leaving an excellent blood trail. From a shooting standpoint, there is no disadvantage in my mind to a high stand. Of course, surrounding foliage will also impact where on the tree you lock the stand in. Because of this, higher is not always better.

CHOOSING A STAND

I used to own one climbing stand, but I gave it to my dad, who uses it during firearms season. To me, climbers are excellent for gun hunting, but I prefer fixed-position treestands for bowhunting. I'm generalizing here, but I find that I have a lot more mobility in most fixed-position stands than I do in a climber. And for a bowhunter, this is critical. I also like the

fact that I don't need a pole-type tree to hunt from like I do with a climber. A fixed-position stand nestled in among the long branches of an oak or pine practically vanishes from sight.

Ladder stands are solid choices for both gun and bowhunting, but most are around 15 feet high. When properly secured to the tree, they offer some safety advantages, since they are easier to climb than the screw-in steps popular with fixed position stand users. Like climbers, ladder stands frequently offer a wrap-around railing that serves as a great gun rest and as a safety device to keep the hunter from falling.

MAKING SHOOTING LANES

Whenever you hunt from a treestand, you have to assess shooting lanes. When using either gun or bow, some surrounding branches usually need to be removed in order to open paths wide enough to areas where deer are likely to pass. There's a balance to be maintained here. I like the camouflage that surrounding cover offers. But there's no worse feeling that having one small twig blocking the vitals of a broadside buck that's becoming more nervous by the nanosecond. I try to give myself at least one option in front, rear, left and right. I've been at this a long time and even when I think I know exactly where the deer are going to

Climbing stands allow you to run and gun. They get you up the tree and hunting faster and can, therefore, help you catch a buck off-guard. Make sure that the climber you choose will accommodate your hunting style and choice of hunting tool.

It does you no good to select the perfect tree, position your stand perfectly and then find yourself without a clear shot because of obstructing brush or branches. Clear a shooting lane front, left, right and rear.

Permanent treestands are dangerous because wood warps over time and nails or screws pull out as trees grow, freeze and thaw. Also, deer tend to associate these stands with human presence and will skirt them whenever they think a hunter might be nearby.

come from, they appear from the opposite direction.

You need three tools for this sort of work. First is a hand-sized trimmer. Those with a ratcheting action ease the effort required to cut branches up to an inch thick. Second, a folding hand saw can be used for larger branches that you can reach from your stand. Always wear a safety belt while you're trimming out a stand. Third, a pole pruner with a saw blade and branch snipper is great for clearing branches up high and out away from your stand.

A hunting buddy can help, pointing out the branches that need clearing while you stay in the stand and do the work. A pole pruner is six feet long but extends to 12 to reach most everything you'll need to worry about.

Remember, don't overdo it. Deer will notice major alterations to the surroundings. Also, it's often illegal to cut branches off trees found on public land. Make sure that you know the regulations where you're hunting. Even if you're on private land, tell the landowner that you'll be removing some branches around your treestand.

KEEP IT QUIET (AND OTHER MAINTENANCE ADVICE)

Last, but not least, a treestand must be quiet. Most of the major treestand manufacturers realize this and go to great lengths to ensure that folding seats and pivot points use nylon bushings or other materials for silence. Often, a squeaky stand is improperly fastened to the tree. Take time to make sure that you've done the job right. The stand should be level and the strap or chain should be tight and secure.

Test your treestands before the season for silence and safety. Even high-quality manufactured stands eventually wear out. Follow the manufacturer's instructions for maintenance immediately after the season, and then check the stand again weeks before the season. That will give you the time to hush any squeaks that might occur.

GROUND BLINDS—NATURALLY

I killed my first buck from the ground with a rifle. In fact, most of the deer that I've killed with a gun have come while I've been hunting from ground blinds; though there wasn't always much of a blind there around me.

I'm very mobile with a portable treestand, but I'm even more mobile with no treestand at all. And where I often gun hunt, in the northern Wisconsin forest, a treestand doesn't always offer a marked increase in the amount of ground that I can cover. In addition, with my trusty Remington .30-06, I don't need the deer close. If I can see them in those woods, they're in range. All I have to do is see them before they see me. So, when I'm gun hunting, I usually hunt from the ground.

In this gun-hunting scenario, I also don't worry a great deal about surrounding cover. I'll usually just search out a thick-trunked tree to back up against or, if there's a good deadfall or top left by the loggers, I'll hide out in there.

Run 'N Gun Ground Blinds

Hunting from the ground for whitetails is becoming less of a disadvantage thanks to better portable ground blinds.

Finding suitable natural ground cover to hide you from a whitetail's eyes is often impossible once you've targeted deer sign to hunt. You can build a blind out of natural cover, of course, but what happens when the deer change their patterns? You have to go build another ground blind. Before you know it, you have forts built around the woods, all of which will crumble in time and none of which will keep the rain or snow off your head.

Commercial ground blinds are really the way to go for serious ground-hunters. Most of the latest models weigh less than 5 pounds and set up in 30 seconds or less with no assembly required. And though few of them are waterproof, most are made of water-resistant nylon and form a shell over the hunter that protects against wind and precipitation.

Sliding fabric drapes are usually incorporated on all sides so that the hunter can shoot no matter where the deer appears. Look for slide-drapes that open silently and allow enough space for you to shoot comfortably. It's wise to keep drapes behind you closed to keep it as dark as possible inside the blind. That way a deer won't be able to recognize your human form inside.

A portable camouflage ground blind properly positioned among other natural cover might offer more concealment than a hunter can achieve by hunting from a tree. Scent, of course, becomes more of an issue, but the movement required to draw a bow or shoulder a gun is hidden better when you're tucked inside one of these blinds.

Many models are available to accommodate two hunters—the perfect means for spending time in the deer woods with a young hunter. Inside a blind, a youngster will be able to stay out longer and get away with movement that would otherwise alert deer. These blinds also allow plenty of room to bring a cooler of snacks to keep your young hunting partner happy while you wait for a whitetail to appear. And kids just love "forts" and hideaways. You'll be making hunting fun!

These commercial blinds from Underbrush, left, and Ameristep, right, are typical of the kind of quality hides you can find on the market. Super-fast setup along with their light weight and superior concealment make these great choices, especially if you want to bring a young hunter along to watch.

During gun season in a forested area, you might actually have a better vantage point from the ground than from a treestand. You can get away with a little more movement there too.

During gun season, deer are usually on the move because, like most other states east of the Mississippi, Wisconsin has a lot of hunters out during a relatively short season. That means I almost always spot the deer before they spot me. I play the wind and keep my eyes peeled.

From the ground I can also usually get a rock-solid rest, because I take the time to stack up some logs or imbed a set of shooting sticks in front of me. The comfort factor is sometimes compromised on the ground. If you're going to

hunt from the ground for hours on end, you need a comfortable chair. Any turkey hunter knows that even the thickest cushions don't work for long when you plant your butt on the ground.

GROUND BLINDS—ARTIFICIALLY

If you're worried about being seen, you can buy a number of excellent commercial blinds that set up and take down literally in seconds. These help break the wind, repel the rain, allow you more freedom of movement and have windows on all sides. They're especially nice if you want to take a young hunter along in the woods with you. Of course, you can also take burlap or other camo material and fashion your own homemade blind, but I bet that your bundle is a lot heavier than those blinds available at your local sporting goods store. Remember, too, that if you're going to hunt from this type of blind during the regular firearms season, it's advisable to attach some kind of blaze-orange flagging to the outside of the blind so that it is visible to other hunters.

These blinds are most critical for bowhunters trying to intercept whitetails on the ground. Getting your bow drawn at eye level against a whitetail is quite a feat. I know some bowhunters who manage to do it on a fairly regular basis because they don't like heights.

Though commercial blinds are available with excellent camo patterns and are small enough to blend into the surroundings relatively well, I'd recommend "brushing up" the blind after you get it in position: Use some of the natural surrounding foliage to break the blind's outline as much as possible, but take care not to allow loose branches to blow against the blind material and create noise on breezy days.

A Note on Permanent Treestands

Since we were just talking maintenance, now is the time to say my peace about permanent treestands. I hate them from just about every angle. They are less effective when it comes to killing deer. A permanent stand is a place whitetails learn to associate with human presence. And that's the last thing you want if you're trying to kill a deer; if that deer you're after is a mature buck, the odds compound against you. Versatility and staying mobile kills deer, and that's why I'm such a fan of commercial portable stands.

Permanent stands are also ugly and unsafe. These eyesores are almost always built from wood that warps over time, after being nailed to tree trunks that grow and expand and contract with temperature extremes. I've heard too many stories of hunters who thought they had built the Taj Mahal of permanent treestands, only to have the thing collapse at the worst possible time. Given the fact that you can buy a topnotch commercial treestand for less than $200, why would you go to the time and effort of building something that won't be as safe or effective? I guess I'll hop off my soapbox. You probably understand where I'm coming from by now.

ONE EXAMPLE

When I was bowhunting in Montana recently, outfitter Doug Gardner and I were looking over a deer trail where one of the guides had spotted a nice buck. The deer was following a fenceline out of the riverbottom, and I'll be darned if there wasn't a single cottonwood fit for a treestand within bow range of that trail. We looked for hours, but there was one spot to kill that buck from and it was on the ground tucked in against that fenceline where a lightning-struck cottonwood was split and fallen down. One side of the fallen tree formed a perfect cave in the tall fenceline grass. I had overhead cover, cover in front, cover at my back and could have cut a couple of nice shooting lanes out to the alfalfa where the trail split. "Could have"; but there was no place for the cameraman to get in the blind. And so we went on to a different spot where we could hang a couple of tree-stands. I don't know if I would have killed that buck on that fenceline, but I sure wouldn't have been against trying it.

THE LAST STAND

You always have to take what the situation gives you, and sometimes the very best place to kill a deer is with both feet planted firmly on the ground. But other times a treestand puts you at a huge advantage. No matter what the scenario, the patient stand-hunter gains the better odds for hunting whitetails successfully.

Sometimes a ground blind is your best choice for getting close to a deer's preferred travel route; you won't always have a suitable tree in the area. By playing the wind and using a portable blind, you can go undetected.

STILL-HUNTING: ART OR IMPOSSIBLE?

Of all the hunting methods illustrated in this chapter, still-hunting is the most difficult to understand. First of all, the name is confusing. "Still" means "not moving," but still-hunting requires movement. *How much* movement is the other big question that is difficult to answer. If one of your buddies at deer camp asked you to demonstrate your still-hunting technique, try to imagine showing him how it is done. Not easy, because the different situations dictate different still-hunting speed.

I remember when I first heard the term just after I started deer hunting. One of the veteran hunters in camp was explaining on the eve of the opener how he was going to stand hunt for the first few hours in the morning and then still-hunt to another stand he had built about a half-mile

away. Since the man explaining his strategy had filled his tag just about every season, I figured that still-hunting was something I better learn how to do—fast! I mean, slow.

SLOW IS THE KEY

Today I rarely still-hunt. In fact, my still-hunting is more scouting than it is hunting. When deer movement is dead during the middle of the Wisconsin firearms season, I'll sometimes slip about the forest, more searching for a new stand site than actually still-hunting. But I have occasionally spotted deer while creeping along and once killed a 6-point buck after spotting him bedded about 75 yards away. I shot him just after he stood up. I'll admit, it was probably more luck than still-hunting skill.

I do remember that day when I was closely studying a number of fresh tracks along a ridgetop and moving along incredibly slowly as I tried to decipher information from the tracks. This head-down approach is not good still-hunting technique, but my snail-like speed was. I remember watching a fishing show on television once and listening to the host explain how to fish a plastic worm for large-mouth bass. He tried to describe how slowly one must inch the worm along in order for the technique to elicit strikes.

"When you think you're fishing it slowly enough," he said, "cut the speed in half and that should be about right."

The same advice, I think, applies well to still-hunting for whitetails. As I pointed out in the stand hunting section of this chapter, whitetails possess eyesight that is designed to detect movement. It stands to reason, therefore, that any deliberate, stealthy hunting gives you a much better chance of seeing a whitetail before it sees you. In fact, you've probably seen this yourself. Have you ever tried to approach a deer that has already seen you? Have you noticed that by moving forward ever so slowly that you can actual-

ly gain ground on an alert deer? This type of movement does not as readily put deer into flight. A quick reach for a slung rifle or fast step forward, though, usually results in a high-speed getaway and a waving white tail.

THE RIGHT CONDITIONS

Later in this chapter we'll talk about tracking, but I want to point out here that a lot of the same conditions required

When still-hunting, your only chance is if you see the deer before he sees you. That means wind in your face, sun at your back and go slow, slow, slow. Look hard, use binoculars.

Stalking is a popular approach in the West, even for whitetail hunters. Quality optics help you find bedded deer after they return from night-time feeding areas.

Spot-&-Stalk Whitetails

I know what you're thinking. If you live along or east of the Mississippi, you've read the headline and said to yourself that this never happens. Well, you're probably right. But whitetails can and are successfully stalked out West every year. And while a bowhunter might not have very good odds of creeping inside 40 yards, a rifleman with good optics and some broken cover to work with can certainly wriggle into rifle range.

The same holds true in the prairie provinces of Canada. *North American Hunter* field editor Jim Shockey spends a lot of his whitetail season trekking across Saskatchewan and Alberta and regularly uses the spot-and-stalk technique that Western hunters employ when pursuing mule deer, elk, pronghorns and bears. Jim makes some important points about the attributes of this approach.

First, of course, you know what you're after from the outset. In a stand-hunting, still-hunting or even a tracking situation, you're waiting for a deer to come to you or for one to appear out of nowhere, probably already within gun range. Your decision then is simply to shoot or not shoot, based on your personal goals and the type of tag in your pocket. On a spot-and-stalk hunt, most of the "hunt" takes place after you've located the animal. And, importantly, after you've had a chance to assess whether or not that is an animal you are interested in harvesting.

Another *North American Hunter* field editor, Mark Kayser, lives in spot-and-stalk South Dakota and often guides whitetail hunters in Montana. To Mark, this is a great test of a big game hunter's skills and an incredibly exciting way to pursue whitetails; especially if you've hunted all your life in forested terrain in the East.

"Whitetails a lot of times just go right out into the middle of a 1,000-acre field," Kayser says. "And you're sitting there scratching your head trying to figure out how you're going to get close to him. That's when you really gotta scrutinize your approach. You have to use whatever cover

Western deer, rather than running for cover, will often head out to the middle of a vast field to avoid danger. In this way they can see for a mile all around. You might just have to wait them out.

you can—irrigation ditches, river banks—but even in those situations, you might only be able to get within 400 or 500 yards. Sometimes you have to wait him out and hopefully he'll come by close enough; otherwise you might be able to call him in. We're talking rutting activity in late October and November, so they'll move a lot if they're not pressured."

Deer hunters in Western states can often take either a mule deer or whitetail on their tag. Kayser said that the spot-and-stalk approach isn't that much different for the two species. "It's not so much the difference in how you go about it, it's the difference in the terrain. No matter what, you have to have the wind in your favor and be out of sight."

Stand hunting can still be an effective tactic in the more open West, and Kayser says he often starts and ends the day on stand when deer movement is at its peak. But when deer movement slows, he gets out and looks for whitetails.

"You can find bedded whitetails," Kayser says. "It's just a matter of easing up into that area and looking at the fringes of those feeding or bedding areas. He might be bedded in a little coulee or in Montana there are a lot of those sage flats. They get in behind a sage bush and it's tough to see them. A lot of times I'll leave the riverbottoms, and a lot of times I'm just blown away by the whitetails I'll find in those high prairie basins."

Kayser likes flat-shooting .30 caliber rifles for this type of deer hunting work, with the .300 Win. Mag. being a favorite of his. Kayser points out that a Western whitetail is well into the 200-pound class, with some pushing 300, and shot distances of 200 yards are average. But more than the rifle, he says, optics can be the key to success.

"You might have to look at a deer from a mile away, and that's difficult to do with some 7-power binoculars," he says.

"Optics are really, really important."

So the next time a fellow deer hunter says that a whitetail can't be stalked, tell him he's wrong. And if you ever get a chance to hunt whitetails west of the Mississippi, you might get to see it for yourself.

To stalk within range of a whitetail you'll need to utilize every available stitch of cover. And you'll probably have to go the long way.

for tracking make for good still-hunting. First off, both techniques are aimed much more at firearms hunters than bowhunters. Getting within bow range of a whitetail on foot, and then being able to draw and shoot undetected, offers worse odds than the lottery. Good luck if you want to try it, but you're better off stand hunting than still-hunting if you're toting a bow.

For firearms hunters considering still-hunting, a thick blanket of soft snow muffles footfalls and is almost necessary, unless the ground cover is wet from a recent rain. If you can hear your footsteps, chances are a whitetail is going to hear you before you get a good look.

Wind can help here as well. Windy days muffle sound and obscure movement, because tree branches and leaves are whipping about. Thus, your movement is well camouflaged. A stout wind also allows you to put your nose squarely into the wind so that any deer out front won't smell you. And if you can take the whitetail's nose out of the equation, you're pretty far along the trail toward success.

A final factor is deer density. In areas with good deer numbers, unless natural deer movement is depressed by poor weather or hunting pressure, I think the vast majority of hunters, even gun hunters, are better off on a well-chosen stand. But where deer populations are lower, covering ground by still-hunting can increase your deer sightings.

An Expert's Perspective

This last component of the equation is likely the one that motivates *North American Hunter* field editor Jim Shockey to hunt afoot often. Shockey (who also provides some thoughts on tracking later in this chapter) does a lot of his whitetail hunting in Saskatchewan, where deer densities are much lower than in most parts of the animal's range in the United States.

"I think it's probably the one method that I've used most effectively," Shockey says. "Still-hunting is great. It's basically a variation on tracking. If the habitat is right, it's just as good as tracking anyway. You have to constantly be aware that there could be a buck in front of you at any time. You know, in bad habitat you go fast, in good habitat you slow down."

Shockey's definition of slow is a lot like the bass fisherman's mentioned earlier. Shockey recounts a successful hunt a decade or so ago in a small woodlot of approximately 30 acres surrounded entirely by field. He says that he was still-hunting along at a pace of about one step per minute.

"It took hours, but I killed him at 14 yards, and he didn't have a clue," Shockey says. "I saw him first. I saw the white hairs on the edge of his tail, and then he flicked it. And then the whole form of his body came through the bush."

When to Still-Hunt

Even if you have all the right conditions with regard to weather and deer numbers, the question of when to still-hunt remains.

Still-hunting success relies on our human vision, which is good at perceiving detail and color. As a result, decent daylight is essential. It does you no good to be afoot the first and last hours of the day, especially in deep woods where you'll have difficulty quickly distinguishing deer from the cover. Sure, good binoculars help and they are must-have gear for still-hunters, but if you have to reach often for your binoculars to scan the forest ahead of you, those whitetail eyes on the lookout for movement will win.

Therefore, mid-morning to mid-afternoon provides the best vision advantage. Even though you might consider these hours the worst for deer hunting, this is where still-hunting can shine.

Still-hunting is best when your footfalls are muffled by snow or wet and windy conditions. With sound eliminated and the wind in your face, it's now a matter of who sees who first.

WHERE TO STILL-HUNT

During the rut, deer are liable to be traveling at any time of the day; so still-hunting during the rut means that you don't have to confine your search to bedding areas. Same is true during firearms seasons. Because of hunting pressure, deer can be up and traveling at any time. Outside of these times, it's more likely that deer will be bedded. But if you know where these bedding areas are and have the weather in your favor, there's nothing wrong with trying to slip into a buck's bedroom.

Though many hunters consider bedding areas sacred ground that should not be disturbed, research has shown that whitetails do return to the same bedding areas even after having been bumped out by humans. And since we're talking about a gun-hunting tactic for the most part, we're talking about relatively short seasons. This means that you might not have the luxury of waiting for the day when you can intercept a deer moving between bed and feed. Other hunters certainly aren't worried about going into "your" bucks' bedrooms.

You might have to go in after him on foot. A bowhunter wouldn't be well-advised to try to sneak into bow range undetected and risk buggering a buck. Armed with a firearm, however, there's nothing wrong with the strategy. Knowing where the deer bed, though, and their likely route of escape is critical in planning your still-hunting approach.

REFINING SPEED

"If I can walk dead quiet, then I can walk a little faster," Shockey says. "There are a whole bunch of factors that come into play. If I can see for 150 yards, there are very few deer that are going to see me before I see them, because you're outside of their sort of defensive range in the forest. I could be anything at that distance. Once you get inside 100 yards, you have to be so much more careful not to let the deer see you or hear you; and this is assuming there is crosswind or wind in your face."

"If I'm hitting a bedding area, that's where I'll slow to a dead crawl and I might stand for half an hour in a spot, maybe longer. You just play your instincts. You'll know when you're hitting good habitat that you should slow right down and maybe the deer will stand up in its bed and you'll see it move."

As Shockey says, still-hunting requires a certain feel for your surroundings, a feel that comes with time spent hunting whitetails on foot at eye level. It can be done. Thousands of deer hunters still-hunt deer successfully every season. Next time the conditions are right, give it a try and see what more it teaches you about the incredible whitetail.

Hunting afoot isn't for everyone. In many cases you are better off on stand. But having the versatility to try something new when the conditions are right makes you a more well-rounded deer hunter.

TRACKING: WHEN, WHERE, HOW?

Some day I will try to track and kill a mature white-tailed buck. If I could do it at all, I'd feel like I'd hit a game-winning grand slam in the deciding game of the World Series. If I could accomplish the feat with my bow, well, I guess I'd feel like I'd conquered big game hunting's most imposing challenge. Yet, while tracking an individual whitetail and eventually harvesting that animal stands at the pinnacle of my challenge measuring stick,

it is the preferred method of many whitetail hunters in North America.

In places like Maine, Saskatchewan, New Brunswick, Alberta, northwestern Montana, northwestern Wisconsin and northern Minnesota, tracking a whitetail might be your very best chance for success. My opinion outside of these areas is that most deer hunters are far better off selecting a high-percentage stand site and waiting for the deer to come to them. Even in some of the tracking meccas listed earlier, my own personal odds might be better waiting on stand. Remember, I've never tracked and harvested a particular deer. Thus, my tracking skills are not skills at all right now. If, however, I committed myself to the art of tracking, and then had the right weather and the right place, I'd be better off afoot than on stand.

THE TRACKING GAME

In an article in a 1997 issue of *North American Hunter*, Bryce Towsley, a resident of Vermont, wrote about the merits of tracking whitetails. He posed a powerful argument.

"Undeniably, the almost universal use of tree-stands and blinds has made us more effective at harvesting deer even though it has blunted our hunting skills," Towsley wrote. "It's just not all that difficult to find a place with lots of fresh deer sign and to wait there for a deer to return... As a result, those valuable old woods skills of generations past are left to rot in our memories. Tracking is one of those hunting art forms that is nearly lost."

Towsley's point is clear. Part of becoming an excellent deer hunter is learning to hunt white-tails successfully in a variety of manners. Versatility. It's critical even in places where stand hunting might usually be the best bet.

Suppose you're in deer camp and it snows 6 or 8 inches overnight. You wake up in the morning and it's windy and cool, but the snow is soft, silent powder. You hunt from your stand the first two hours of daylight, but nothing's moving. On your way back to the truck you cut a fresh set of wide tracks in the snow. Looks like a buck, and a big one at that. You can track him. Or you can wait for a day when the deer return to their normal travels so that you can head back to your stand.

It can happen. It even happened to me once in December in Mississippi; an honest 8 inches of snow overnight. Instead of getting on a track, though, I waited for normal weather to return. I should have been tracking.

A BUCK AT THE END OF THE TRAIL

"Every single time there's fresh snow, I'll be out there the next morning putting on miles until I find a big track and I'll go on that every single time," says *North American Hunter* field editor Jim Shockey. "The whole day is anticipation. He could be there at any single step you take. You know absolutely 100 percent that there's a buck at the end of that track. What

more of a guarantee could you ever want on a hunt? I could sit there all day on a stand and never know if a buck's going to come by or if there's even a buck there in the whole general area. But when I'm on a track there is a buck there, and he's somewhere ahead of me. That's the one sure thing about tracking. And I'll take a sure thing any day on deer. Goodness knows, you rely on luck so many other times."

Though Shockey spends most of his whitetail hunting days in the big buck Canadian provinces of Alberta and Saskatchewan, he says that the tactic can work outside of the more traditional tracking areas I mentioned earlier. Like my Mississippi experience that one December, Shockey recalls a tailor-made tracking day on a past hunt in Iowa.

Reading a track will tell you when to speed up and when to slow down. In open country, you must scrutinize the cover ahead to search for a buck watching his back-trail.

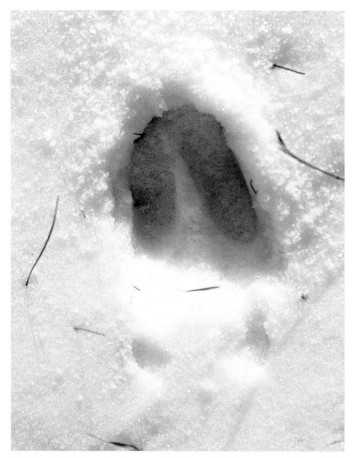

Buck or doe? Some hunters would tell you that they can say for certain by this single track. Others look for more signs to determine whether or not they are following the right track.

Drag marks between tracks are, to many hunters, an indication of a buck track. When he's moving quickly like this, you might have to move along at a trot in order to find him before dark.

"I hunted for 10 days, and there was snow on the ground, but it was crunchy and it was a tough hunt at that point," Shockey says. "The last day we finally got some snow, and I happened to catch the worst cold I've had. The cold didn't kill me. What killed me was lying in bed knowing there was snow on the ground and that finally I had the advantage on the deer. If I wouldn't have gotten one, I would have had a lot more fun than I had the previous nine days waiting for that one day of opportunity. They don't fly down there that I know of. They make tracks, you follow them."

THE RIGHT CONDITIONS

Like Shockey said, tracking conditions have to be right no matter where you are hunting. If he could construct the perfect day for tracking, he'd get 4 inches of fresh, powdery snow with a total snow depth of about 8 inches. He doesn't want any part of the snowpack to be crusty and loud. And with 8 inches of depth to work with, even if he steps on and breaks a branch, the snow will conceal any sound.

"I'm moving through the forest quiet as a mouse," Shockey says. "Deer literally cannot hear me. Their ears are good, but they're not good enough to hear someone in

8 inches of snow with proper gear on. I'm not too worried about if it's the rut or not the rut, because at the end of that track there's a buck. I don't need wind or snow falling. I'll kill that buck if I have enough time, as long as I don't hit a fence where I can't hunt. That's the other thing. You need the spaces where you can walk 10 miles if you need to."

This consideration is the reason that some of those regions mentioned above are prime tracking country. State or provincial forest country might cover tens of thousands of acres, eliminating any concern of encountering access barriers while on track.

Big woods country at the northern fringes of the whitetail's range also has a lower carrying capacity than the farm country farther south in the United States. Lower-quality forage, severe winters and wolves keep whitetail populations to less than 10 deer per square mile in some of these areas. That means that when you get on a snowy track, it's easier to stay on that track, because you won't lose it in a maze of other deer tracks. And, since most whitetail hunters willing to put in the work to track a whitetail are after mature bucks, it's important to stay on the buck track you find at the start of the day. Thus, lower deer densities are better.

Cruising logging roads or other "edges" is the way to locate a track to start on for the day. Of course, it's not bad to get a look at the actual deer that you'll be tracking! Most times, though, you have to pick a set of tracks and go with it.

BUCK OR DOE?

Telling a buck track from a doe track, despite all you might have read, isn't as difficult as you might believe. In the North, most mature bucks will outweigh does by at least 100 pounds. That means they'll leave a bigger track, of course, but also, the distance between their tracks will be greater, because an average buck is wider across his body and longer than a doe. And even if you're not a tracker, after you've looked at a lot of deer tracks you get a feel for which ones are

bucks and which ones are does. Attitude is something that Shockey looks for in a track.

"I love to see a track that I can put my four fingers in and not touch the sides on it," Shockey says. "It helps you stay disciplined on the hunt all day long. Our bucks are a factor bigger in size than a doe. Their tracks are bigger than a doe."

"All that said, the size of the track is probably the least important way to tell whether I'm on a buck track or a doe track. I don't need to know the width of the track to know that it's a buck. You can tell that by what the deer's doing. Is

it sort of wandering here and there, sort of feeding? Bucks aren't going to do that; not when there's snow on the ground. They're rutting. He's moving across country. He's not goofing around and wandering. If he is, he's probably a small buck. A big buck, during the rut—you can tell that whatever made that is just swaggering. And also where the track is. Where it's moving through. Does don't necessarily go the same places the bucks do."

THE STARTING LINE

Sounds good so far, right? But where do we begin that day when the conditions are just right?

Shockey says he starts off by covering ground early in the morning around the perimeter of the area he's selected to hunt. He says that a swamp edge or fenceline might be his guide as he searches for a track that he wants to follow. It could also be an old logging road—anything that will help him to move along quickly without walking over any of the same area. This search might take him a mile, maybe even two or three before the tracking ever begins. Again, Shockey points out that it doesn't have to be a monster track to get him started.

"I don't care what size he is right off the bat," Shockey says. "Now, obviously, I'd prefer a big track, but if we're starting to get 10 in the morning, I'm going to go on whatever track I find that I know is a buck track. I'm not going to worry about the size of it at that point, because the buck that made that track is going to take me to every bedding area, and that means he's going to take me to every hot doe that has the biggest buck with that hot doe. And I don't necessarily need to kill the buck that made the track, but I will possibly kill a buck that is with the doe.

"So that track will take me to other deer in other areas and maybe a bigger track. Just for my own men-

You must be comfortable in your surroundings with little fear of getting lost—and with the skills and equipment to spend a night in the woods if necessary. A track in some regions might take you several miles. Only you can decide whether the rewards are worth it.

tal discipline and motivation, I prefer to think that I'm on the track of a big deer. I'll try to tell them apart, but you cannot tell what kind of a rack the buck has—impossible. I mean, some of the biggest deer I've seen or killed have these big, heavy 4-point racks that don't score worth beans, but they're the bull of the woods. But some of the biggest racks I've seen were on smaller-bodied deer."

OTHER CONSIDERATIONS

Physical conditioning, if you haven't already guessed, is essential in successful tracking. Not only might you cover a couple of miles just searching for a promising track, that track might lead you another several miles before you encounter the buck. Shockey says that he's covered as many as six miles on a particular buck track.

Depending on what the track tells him, Shockey might be jogging along the track or hardly moving at all. This is where tracking experience comes into play and helps you spot the buck before he spots you. Shockey remembers one buck that he killed just after the deer stood from its bed. "I knew he was close because the tracks started to fade and wander and cut off to the side," he says.

Shockey says that wind isn't typically a major consideration because he hasn't often encountered bucks tail-winding or walking with the wind. He adds that he usually finds the bucks he's tracking bedded on spots where they can see some distance around them.

"Once I see that wandering where it looks like he's getting tired, then I start looking at the far side of clearings where he can look back, on a knob, you know," Shockey says. "I'll be at a fast pace, but when he starts to slow down, I don't know if he's one hour ahead of me or one minute ahead of me. But once he starts going again, I'm traveling fast again. You'll start to sense when he's about to do something different than he's been doing. Then you have to slow down to about a step every minute and be thinking about

where he's going to be bedded. 'Where could he be right now in front of me?' And if you're doing that you've got an advantage."

TRACKING LESSONS

Tracking teaches you how to track, but it also teaches you more about deer than you can learn on stand. Think about it like this. Imagine that you could be, excuse the metaphor, a

He's out there, somewhere. With access to thousands of acres in front of you, it's a matter of trying to find him before dark. Move quickly but carefully.

tick on a buck's back. Imagine that you could take every single step with him for an entire day. And now imagine the insights such a journey might give you as a deer hunter. That, says Shockey, is one of his main motivations for tracking whitetails.

"You spend one day on a track and you'll know more about the country and what the deer are doing," Shockey says. "You'll find places in there that you never had any idea about. You thought you knew the ground like the back of your hand; you don't know it at all until you get on a track for a day. You stay hard on a buck track, it'll take you all kinds of places. And on top of that, the whole day is a lesson in deer behavior—what they're doing, where they're moving."

Say you get on a track that turns out to be a doe. Again, Shockey says, there is value in tracking that deer. Odds are good that any track will lead you to other deer, or at least to areas that other deer are using at any given time. During most general firearms seasons, when the deer seem to vanish after the first day or two of the hunt, that's valuable information to have. It might help you unravel how the deer are avoiding all the other hunters in the area.

"In Minnesota one season, I followed a track for three miles and I learned where these deer were hiding because I followed the track," Shockey says. "They were in this waist-high brush that I never would have expected there'd be a deer, yet that's where the tracks kept going into, and I kept bumping deer out of these little tiny 20-yard-wide patches of brush. That's how they were avoiding all the gun hunters. So I didn't get a deer, but I sure knew where to set up to kill a deer at that point."

Shockey adds: "Any time is a good time to track. If I've got fresh snow on the ground, I'm tracking. The very least you're going to do is learn a lot more about the deer and what they're doing right now, not what they were doing before the season. I know what they're doing today, and they're probably going to be doing that again tomorrow. So at the very worst, I spent a day learning, so that's a well-spent day in my mind compared to sitting in a stand knowing nothing."

North American Hunter field editor Jim Shockey loves to track whitetails. He says he learns more in a day of tracking than he might learn in many weeks sitting on stand. And while he's working the trail, he knows there's a buck somewhere ahead.

The Well-Dressed Tracker

The same day, with the same weather, requires the stand hunter and the tracker to dress very differently. On stand during a 10°F day, the hunter needs heavy pac boots and four or five layers to be able to hunt most of the day in comfort. The tracker, on the other hand, is moving and doesn't need nearly as much insulation. The tracker also needs specialized footwear and outerwear to be able to sneak close and spot a whitetail before it spots him.

Shockey wears the same type of footwear no matter if the temperature is 30°F or minus 20°F. His choice is unconventional, to say the least, but effective. It consists of a pair of wool socks against the skin, then a heavy-duty pulled raw wool knitted sock that is approximately 1 inch thick. Shockey buys these from a supplier in northern Saskatchewan. The thick sock, which is incredibly quiet, comes up almost to the knee and over the top of whatever clothing you're wearing on your legs. Over the thick sock, Shockey wears moccasin rubbers that come up to his ankle. These are thin rubber and the sole is a bit textured for grip.

He explains that the sock on the outside will accumulate some snow but that the insulating qualities of the thick sock keep the snow on the outside from melting and hold the heat on the inside. As a result, Shockey often leaves this thick outer sock outside overnight so that it doesn't get wet. He only brings it inside if he is certain that he can get the sock totally thawed and dry before the next day's hunt.

"Using that right up to 20°F below, I can walk all day long," Shockey says. "I can sit for probably an hour; but if you're moving, you want fast and light."

And, of course, quiet. Shockey says he, like many deer hunters, prefers fleece for its silent qualities. Therefore, fleece jackets and pants are his choice in outerwear.

Other items to consider for a day of deer tracking include a hand-held GPS unit, topographical map of the area, fire-starting kit, compass and space blanket. A deer track can take you places in the deer woods you've never been before. If you have a deep fear of getting lost or of not being able to fend for yourself overnight in case you do, you might be better off on stand.

If, however, you're confident in your knowledge of the terrain and your woods skills, then you might want to try deer hunting's ultimate challenge of tracking. Whether or not you ever succeed in your quest of tracking and taking a whitetail, the knowledge you gain in the pursuit will undoubtedly help you successfully hunt whitetails.

Shockey with a big, old drop-tine buck that the Saskatchewan locals had given up for gone. After a couple days of following his track, Shockey got inside the buck's head, worked himself one step ahead, and here proudly holds the reward.

THE DEER DRIVE

Everything preceding in this chapter discussed your locating and successfully hunting whitetails by taking advantage of their natural movements and habits: stand hunting, still-hunting and tracking all rely on our abilities to find the deer before it finds us. Sadly, we often fail. Deer, as a hunting friend of mine once said, have radar. Even when the wind is right, the stand is right, the camouflage is right, the deer can somehow make everything go wrong for you. Some hunters call it the sixth sense. Call it what you will; whitetails certainly have a way of finding us out.

ground, while hunters pass within 10 yards or less. It might go out the back, between the drivers, before they have a chance to react. Or it might react as predicted, only to have the stander miss the full-tilt whitetail as it flashes through an opening.

North American Hunter field editor Jim Shockey has been involved in a number of deer drives since his youth in Saskatchewan. Where deer densities are low, or when deer movement is suppressed by hunting pressure or poor weather, deer drives are often the best option available. Shockey says that, more than numbers of hunters in your team, every participant has to understand what it takes to conduct a successful deer drive. And everyone has to believe that each drive is going to produce. Because as soon as you let your guard down, the deer has the upper hand.

"It doesn't matter the number of people," Shockey says. "It's that either the standers or drivers don't believe that it's going to work. So every drive has to be set up as if there's a big deer in there. Too many guys get lazy. They don't believe, so they'll drive the standers over and, you know, bang the doors, 'See you in an hour' and then the guy crunches over to wherever he's supposed to wait. Then the truck drives around the far side, and the guys all get out bang, bang, bang with the doors. Well, I mean, these deer can't add two plus two, but they're not exactly idiots as to what's going on around them. And I think that's where most deer drives fail. If you can set your standers up without the deer knowing, that's vital. So they have to slip in there assuming there's a deer in there that could be on the edge watching. And the drivers—same thing."

TAKE IT SERIOUSLY

Stealth still matters, despite the definition of a deer drive being forced movement. You still, as Shockey points out, need the deer to go where you want them to go in order to be successful. And if you show your hand ahead of time, you lose. In fact, Shockey says that he likes to get the standers set downwind of the cover that's going to be pushed, and then wait for an hour or two before the drivers move in. That way, if the deer did notice something out of place, enough time has passed for them to settle down and forget any minor disturbance.

"If he suspects there's something going on at that end (standers), why would he even leave the bush? Why would he even stand up?" Shockey asks.

It's a good point since a lot of drives are conducted after a hunter has spotted a buck enter a particular woodlot or patch of cover. Yet, even after the drivers move through, the deer never appears. The hunters assume the buck vanished before everyone got into position, but he might still be bellied down in the cover. Shockey says that large patches of cover require a stander out "the back door" in case the deer decides to double back. From there it's a matter of knowing the lay of the land and the escape routes that the whitetails use in a certain situation. This comes with experience of driving particular

Thus, the deer drive. No secrets. No need for a perfectly placed stand. No need to fret about snapping a twig underfoot. It's forced movement. It's letting the deer know that danger is approaching from one location in the hope that this will force them to move to another location. In between, we put other hunters charged with the task of tagging these whitetails before they can reach sanctuary.

GAMES DEER (AND HUNTERS) PLAY

But even with large groups of 10 or more hunters, a single whitetail often ends up with the upper hand. It might lay low in the face of approaching danger, chin pinned to the

More often than not, they'll bust out where you least expect them. Successful deer drives plan ahead for deer slipping out the back or finding other unexpected escapes.

patches of cover over and over again.

"There are still patches that I pushed as a youngster," Shockey says, "and 30 years later they're still pushing deer out of there. I hunted there this last year, and we were pushing the same exact sloughs that we pushed when I was a kid and the deer were doing the same exact thing."

A CASE FOR SMALL GROUPS

Too many drivers can spoil a setup. Shockey doesn't like loud, aggressive drives, because the noise gives away the position of the hunters and gives the deer reference for escape. Thus, fewer hunters (if they work the right cover diligently) can sometimes more efficiently nudge deer in front of their partners.

In northern Wisconsin a few years ago, my brother-in-law, Mike Vogel, had a bow tag open, and we tried to push some small patches of cedar swamp midday. Knowing the lay of the northern forest land well from hunting there for many years, we set up in known travel funnels and played the wind to our advantage.

Mike was waiting on ridge along a swamp when I pushed a 6-point buck within 10 yards of the tree Mike huddled behind. His arrow did the job and he filled his tag thanks to the most simple of deer drives. Two men and one bow. Like

anything else in deer hunting, the more experience you have in hunting the local whitetails, the better your ability to anticipate what they'll do next. And that's vital in successfully hunting whitetails.

It's not uncommon for whitetails to hold tight as a rabbit when a deer drive is approaching. The drivers have to be observant and not just plow ahead toward the standers.

The standers must slip into their positions undetected. In fact, it's wise to let them sit for an hour before beginning the drive so that the deer have settled down and are more likely to exit as predicted.

Chapter 5

DEER HUNTING TOOLS

How many times have you been there, right at the moment of truth, when something went wrong with your gun or bow? It made a noise and spooked the deer. You couldn't see the deer through your scope. Your gun wouldn't fire for some reason. The sights got knocked out of alignment.

It's happened to me, and I've heard a lot of horror stories from fellow hunters. Fortunately, firearms and bow manufacturers continue to churn out better products every year, thereby reducing the risk of a miss or missed opportunity.

The hard part in deer hunting is getting to the point where the shot finally presents itself. All the work leading up to the shot is the stuff that requires the dedication and perseverance. That's why it hurts all the more when you've done everything perfectly, only to have a shot opportunity go awry.

In this chapter we'll discuss some of the latest in the deer hunting tools at our disposal. We'll make sure you're doing everything possible to make your hard-earned shot count. We'll provide some guidelines

In well-trained hands, an effective deer-hunting tool need not be the most powerful or high-tech.

on calibers, effective range and accessories. We'll even help you pack your daypack with all the essentials.

So no matter if you're a bowhunter, rifleman, slug gun hunter, blackpowder enthusiast or handgunner, you'll find advice on your chosen hunting tool. Maybe you're into all of the above, in which case you get to enjoy all of the whitetail hunting opportunities available in your state and across the animal's range.

The more you hunt, after all, the more you learn about successfully hunting whitetails.

THE WHITETAIL RIFLE

Some writers would argue that you can't confine this topic to a single section within a book on whitetail hunting. They'd suggest that this is a subject better dealt with in a book of its own. Certainly, there are books already written on this topic. I say that there has been a lot of paper wasted and a lot of time lost arguing the merits of the .30-30 Win. or pitting the .270 Win. against the .30-06.

Most of this is simply stuff for gun nuts to gab about because they like to gab about such things. And that's fine.

But listen, a deer rifle and the ammunition that I choose for it need to do only one thing—kill a deer quickly and humanely.

As side benefits I like as little noise and recoil as possible, but the bottom line is that I want to be able to consistently put a good bullet in a deer's vitals. Ballistic coefficients, velocities, glass-bedding and all that other stuff doesn't do much for me. If that's what you're looking for, there are a pile of thick books out there to turn your crank.

The rest of this section will be devoted to the *practical* side of deer rifles. We'll outline a range of calibers that are reasonable for the work at hand, talk about regions where particular rifles and calibers are most suitable, and discuss some of the attributes that make deer rifles work well in the field.

DEFINING A DEER RIFLE

Years ago, the definition of "deer rifle" was a lot simpler: A lever-action .30-30 Win. The end. Today a lot of gun writers pay mostly disrespect to the venerable .30-30 Win. It will still meet the definition in this book, but there are better choices for most whitetail hunters. Really, we're talking more about calibers right now than the rifles themselves. Most deer rifles available today come in a wide range of calibers. And caliber is really more important than the rifle itself when you're talking about hunting performance.

At the lower end of the deer caliber spectrum are those like the .243 Win., 6mm Rem. and .25-06 Rem. Of course, state game regulations might also dictate minimum calibers for deer hunting.

If you have the option of using calibers like the .243 Win., 6mm Rem. and .25-06 Rem., I'll refer you quickly back to the second section in this book, "Deer Hunting Discipline." These calibers, especially, require you to clearly recognize the maximum effective range and never exceed it. Most veteran deer hunters who I know recommend 1,000 foot-pounds as a minimum amount of energy required to cleanly take a white-tailed deer. Cartridges loaded for these calibers utilize light bullets weighing between 100 and 120 grains. And the 1,000 foot-pound energy minimum is met at relatively modest distances. You should reference ammunition information available in books or on Web sites from ammo manufacturers to determine where your load falls below 1,000 foot-pounds. That is your maximum range, no ifs, ands or buts about it.

At the upper end, well, there really is no upper end, because dead is dead, as the saying goes. If you don't mind the weight, recoil and muzzle blast of a .300 magnum, then it will certainly do a fine job at humanely killing whitetails. I know a lot of deer hunters who actually choose .300 magnums on occasion for whitetails. One of them is *North American Hunter* Shooting Advisory Council Member Bryce Towsley.

NAHC Member Sherry Fears with a great Texas buck she downed with a Thompson/Center single-shot rifle. No matter what your choice in action or caliber, the keys are to learn to shoot it well, and recognize both your own and the rifle's limitations.

Bolt rifles are noted for their reliability and accuracy. Though the battle-scarred rig on the left won't win any style points, it scores high with this happy hunter and certainly did the job on a very nice buck.

"I like the .300s, but I think there are a couple of qualifiers. Number one is that you be able to shoot them well," Towsley says. "The other qualifier is that you use good bullets. I don't believe that you can overkill a deer. The magnums might be a bit excessive in some minds, but I like the increased punch and flatter trajectory particularly for trophy deer hunting. If you're going to travel somewhere and hunt trophy deer, that extra margin is important."

Towsley recommends top-shelf, premium ammunition for the .300 magnums when using these on deer. He says that the magnums have a reputation of being overly destructive on deer-sized game, but that this reputation is formed because many hunters have chosen soft bullets that don't hold up at high velocities. The Winchester FailSafe and Nosler Partition are a couple of bullets that Towsley holds in high regard.

From a practicality standpoint, if you think that you need a magnum in your deer hunting arsenal, a .300 Win. Mag. is probably the best choice for most hunters. For those who'll be doing most of their whitetail hunting in the West, a flatter shooter like the .300 Wthby Mag. or new Remington .300 Ultra Mag. are better options.

You really don't need to go any further than this at the upper end of the energy scale. Some deer hunters, as Towsley points out, will say that these calibers are overkill. And in a lot of deer hunting situations, you surely don't need this much gun. But if you hunt in the North, especially the prairie provinces of Canada, where 300-pound bucks are not uncommon, or out West where 300-yard shots are not uncommon, a .300 is not unreasonable.

CHOOSING AN ACTION

A white-tailed deer doesn't care much what rifle action you choose. If you can shoot well with a pump, autoloader, lever action, single-shot or bolt, use it! But here are some guidelines in case you are trying to decide what might fit your needs best.

Bolt Action

North American Hunting Club Executive Director Bill Miller, as many of you are probably aware, appreciates precision in his rifles. He likes to handload his own rifle cartridges in an attempt to produce more consistent, accurate rounds, and he measures his groups to the tenth of an inch. He's also a dyed-the-wool deer hunter who has tagged his share of whitetails with a broad range of rifle calibers and actions. His choice in action?

"The bolt action gets my nod," Bill says, "They are rifle-to-rifle the most accurate. They are rifle-to-rifle the most reliable. I own a pump and several lever actions, but were I to own and hunt with only one deer rifle, it would be a bolt action."

As Bill says, a bolt is a good choice no matter where you hunt whitetails. Because of the popularity of this action, most manufacturers offer models in a wide range of chamberings, so finding one in your favorite caliber is seldom a problem. A bolt probably shines most in the West, in Texas and in the prairie provinces of Canada where whitetails can frequently be targeted at 300 yards and beyond. There is no disputing that the bolt is the king in the accuracy category. So at these longer ranges, the average hunter can more consistently group bullets in the kill zone than he can with rifles in other actions.

Pumps, Autos & Levers

In places where a 100-yard shot is a long shot because of the habitat, pumps, autoloaders and levers stack up just fine in the accuracy department. It doesn't much matter if your Remington pump only shoots a 2-inch group at 100 yards compared to your buddy's Browning bolt turning out 1-inch groups. A deer's vital chest area is a good 8 inches in diameter. It's fun to shoot super-tight groups at the range, but hunting accuracy and bench-rest accuracy are two different things.

Don't get the wrong idea. I'm all for the most accurate rifle rig

possible. But from a treestand at 75 yards in the wind and cold with a nice buck walking slowly through the cover, benchrest groups are out the window. Now it's down to the hunter. The guy with the pump who shoots the 2- or 3-inch 100-yard group at the range might have killed 20 bucks with that same rifle and knows "how" to shoot it. And, because of his experience as a hunter, he might do a lot better in this situation than the rookie deer hunter with the one-hole bolt.

See what I'm saying? Most modern, scoped rifles are pretty precise hunting tools. What's in the rifle is not nearly so important as what's in the hunter.

Bill said it another way in one of the "Hunting Guns, Ammo and Optics" columns he wrote in *North American Hunter* some time ago:

"The best deer gun is the one that you've shot a great deal—the more, the better," Bill wrote. "It's a gun in which you've invested the time and money to make sure that it fits you well and, therefore, it feels as natural as your own limbs. It's a gun that has consistently produced quick, one-shot kills in the conditions under which you hunt most. It's a gun that you cherish but would retire to the safe if a new one could be proven to do the job better."

Scoping It Up

Deer rifles and scopes go hand-in-hand. It's rare to see a deer hunter anymore with a scopeless rifle. And that's a good thing.

Every deer hunter can benefit from having a quality scope mounted on his rifle's receiver. A scope helps you aim more precisely and to see the sight picture much more clearly—especially during low-light situations early and late in the day when so many whitetails are harvested.

A top-notch scope might cost you nearly as much as the rifle you mount it on.

We don't have space here to go into all the characteristics of a typical riflescope. But we'll concentrate on some of the main things to consider if you're in the market for a scope.

Quality

Many deer hunters still are willing to spend $500 or more on a topnotch deer rifle only to top it off with a low quality scope. It's been said before, but bears repeating: good optics are as important as a good rifle. In other words, it's not out of the question to spend as much on a riflescope as you would on the rifle itself. All you have to do is compare what you see through a $100 scope versus a $500 or $700 scope. You can see the difference. It might not be readily apparent inside a sporting goods store, but it will be during those low-light conditions or when it's raining or snowing in your deer stand.

Magnification

Next consideration is magnification. The 3-9X variable power scope is probably the most popular. However, I really wonder how many whitetails are shot with the scope set on 9X. Most Eastern deer hunters don't need that upper magnification range. A 2-7X or even a fixed power scope in something like 4X will serve most deer hunters, who won't get shot opportunities past 200 yards.

No matter what kind of magnification you settle on, if you select a variable, keep the power ring turned down to the lower end, 3X or 4X, until you find the deer in your scope. In many cases you'll find that you have all the magnification you need right there and that the wider sight picture provided by low-power magnification makes it much easier to locate the deer in your scope. If you want more magnification after you locate the deer, it's a simple matter to adjust the power ring as you keep the deer in your crosshairs.

Mounting

Finally, mounting the scope is critical. You can buy an excellent scope and handicap yourself with a shoddy mounting job. Mounting a scope is not difficult, but it's probably better left to a professional at a gun shop. Quality bases and rings are as important as a quality scope. And getting the tube secured rock-solid within the mounts is crucial. As a general rule, mount the scope as close to the rifle's barrel as possible without it touching. The lowest bases allow the least chance that the scope moves at all as it rides atop the barrel.

The forces of recoil test a scope's mounting. So do impacts that scopes sustain in transport and during hunting. The farther a scope rides above the receiver, the more likely it is to shift, albeit slightly, as a result of these forces.

I see some big-woods hunters who use the "shoot-through" style bases that are supposed to allow aiming with the open sights if a deer is on the move or the hunter cannot locate the deer in his scope for whatever reason. A couple of hunters in our deer camp have used these for a number of seasons but have yet to utilize the "shoot-through" option. Plus, they've had some problems keeping their scopes zeroed with these very high mounts. Thus, they're coming off in favor of standard bases.

I think you too will find that once you've hunted whitetails with a quality riflescope, you'll never go back to rifle sights.

In brush and shadows like this, it's impossible for the human eye to pick out intervening objects at any distance. That's where a good scope earns its keep.

THE OTHER GUNS

As I mentioned earlier, confining modern rifles to a few pages within this book is difficult. But then I realized that a lot of gun writers have written a lot of books on the guns themselves. And I really don't need to walk those same trails all over again. The same goes for muzzleloaders, slug guns and hunting handguns. Each of these hunting tools could justify a book unto itself, but the focus of this book is to help you hunt whitetails successfully. And to do that, you don't necessarily need to know all of the inner workings of your hunting tool. It doesn't hurt, of course, but the imperative is that you select the right tool for the job and then learn how to use it well.

With that goal in mind, I've called a few gun-writer friends, who also are avid, accomplished deer hunters. With their help, we'll get to the nuts and bolts of "the other guns," which really are *the* guns as far as a lot of deer hunters are concerned. One of my friends, who I interview later in this chapter, Dave Henderson of Endicott, New York, points out that 3.9 million deer hunters use slug guns. And given the proliferation of whitetails across most of the animal's range, special seasons for blackpowder and handgunners have resulted in growth in these areas as well.

All these hunting tools have one thing in common: they require more discipline from the deer hunter who uses them. They do not perform (maybe with the exception of some of the pistols chambered for rifle cartridges) nearly as efficiently or as accurately as their long gun centerfire rifle counterparts. That, in fact, is the reason why a lot of deer hunters choose these tools when choice is an option—increased challenge. Forcing yourself to get closer to deer inevitably makes you a better deer hunter. And having more deer hunting tools at your disposal makes for longer seasons and more deer hunting opportunity. If you're like me, the longer the deer season the better!

So let's broaden our horizons on "the other guns."

SLUG GUNS

I can remember my first attempt at sighting-in my old smoothbore Savage 20 gauge pump with slugs. I can't remember what type of ammunition I was using, but I clearly remember scattering slugs around a 2-foot diameter target at 30 steps. It never was "sighted-in." When we moved deer camp to the northern part of Wisconsin and rifle country the next season, I was thrilled to tote a scope-sighted .30-06 instead of my bird gun.

What I missed in the next 10 years of hunting up North, though, was vast improvement in the slug guns that my buddies were using down in the southern farm country region of the state. In fact, they started talking about making accurate 100-yard shots with their new, high-tech slug guns.

"It's been the fastest growing area in all of shooting by far," Henderson says. "One analogy I've been using is that if flight had progressed at the same pace as slug gun technology, they would have launched the space

shuttle about 10 years after Kitty Hawk. About 20 years ago, if you had a slug gun that could hit a gallon can three times in a row at 50 yards, that was a tack driver. I've shot a half-inch five-shot [100-yard] group. I've shot probably two dozen 1-inch groups and that's with commercial ammunition, but from a custom gun and on a perfect day with the right lot number and wind."

Henderson is quick to point out that slug guns, despite the vast improvement, are still 100-yard hunting tools. A slug fired from a gun held parallel to the ground and five feet off the ground, will fall to the earth only 240 yards away. And kinet-

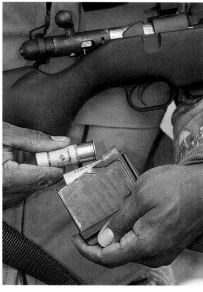

Slug gun hunters have vastly better firearms and ammunition to work with today than they did 20 years ago.

Despite incredible accuracy, slug guns have gained, they remain 100-yard hunting tools. Inside that range, they are nearly as reliable as centerfire rifles.

ic energy falls below the 1,000 foot-pounds level at ranges just outside 100 yards. The 1,000 foot-pound level is an accepted minimum for taking deer-sized game cleanly. And then there's the wind.

"A little bit of wind makes a big difference because slugs are so slow," Henderson says. "An 8 mph cross-wind, which is really just a gentle breeze, puts you two inches off center at 50 yards and six to eight inches at 100 yards. A .270 Win. will be off less than a quarter inch at 100 yards under the same conditions. Another thing is that it takes so long for the slug to get out of the barrel that the gun recoils a half an inch. So barrel movement can make a big difference."

Despite some of the incredible groups Henderson has shot on perfect days with custom guns, he says that the average deer hunter should be happy with a slug gun that will group inside 4 inches at 100 yards on a decent day. He adds that accuracy is improved in some of the bolt-action slug gun models available from companies like Marlin, Savage and Mossberg.

Henderson says that the new ammunition on the market also has been a boon to slug gun hunters. He points especially to the Federal Barnes Expander ammunition and

Remington's improved CopperSolid. Henderson says that these are more like bullets than slugs and, therefore, shoot more accurately than many of the early sabot/slug combinations. They also are designed to mush to double their diameter for excellent on-game performance.

Many of the special-purpose shotguns currently available with interchangeable choke tubes offer a rifled tube option so that a hunter can use the same gun for all his bird hunting and deer hunting. Yet, Henderson says the fully-rifled barrels do a better job of spinning slugs and maintaining accuracy beyond 50 yards. A fully-rifled barrel to fit many of these special-purpose guns is often an option and probably a better one than going with the rifled tube.

Henderson says that slug gun-only hunting areas will probably increase in the coming years as humans encroach farther into whitetail country. In fact, he believes that eastern Pennsylvania—traditional rifleman's country—will soon be slug gun-only. *North American Hunter's* "Whitetails" columnist Larry Weishuhn agrees with the overall assessment.

"I think we're going to see that as we increase our metropolitan areas," Weishuhn says. "It's something that we're going to have to contend with. Deer populations are going to increase, and people will have to realize that hunting is going to have to change. Even here in Texas, now there are some bowhunting and some shotgun slug hunting opportunities because the projectiles don't travel as far as a rifle bullet."

HANDGUNS

The same close-range thinking applies to handguns, but only in the revolver realm when we're talking deer guns. The single-shot and bolt-action pistols chambered for the rifle cartridges are a whole different animal and one discussed a little later.

In the world of revolvers, the "real" handguns in the eyes of many hunters, the first order of business is settling on a caliber that is suitable for whitetails. The .357 Rem. Mag. has been a caliber of intense debate during the years, but Weishuhn and *NAH* Shooting Advisory Council Member Bryce Towsley both agree that it's not suitable for whitetails.

"The .357 Rem. Mag. certainly kills animals, and with the

Farm country and more populated regions often limit deer hunters to shotguns only. In fact, more states are expanding shotgun-only zones, which has increased hunters' demands for top-quality gear.

Larry Weishuhn's ever-present cowboy hat is more than just for looks. It's been called to action as a rest more than once as it is here, cradling a Thompson/Center handgun.

Partition Gold ammunition from Winchester it's even better, but the .44 Rem. Mag. is my personal minimum for a deer hunting handgun," Weishuhn says. "The maximum effective range is about 75 yards."

"I certainly don't think a .357 Rem. Mag. is a deer gun, and that is where the controversy is," Towsley says. "I would put the minimum in a revolver at .41 Rem. Mag., but since that's all but dead and buried, my personal minimum is a .44 Rem. Mag."

Towsley says that he really likes the bigger .454 Casull, though he admits it might be a little much for deer. But with Winchester's Partition Gold handgun ammo, Towsley likes the increased energy.

Both Towsley and Weishuhn recommend an optical aiming device over open sights, even though these revolvers are 75-yard tools. Light-gathering ability of a traditional scope or the target acquisition of a red dot sight help a hunter shoot more accurately in less time—an important consideration in close-range work.

Still, learning to shoot a revolver accurately requires time and dedication similar to bowhunting. Of course, there are two ways to look at this. Some deer hunters see it as a hindrance, others as another challenge to be conquered in their quest to become more well-rounded deer hunters.

"The mental aspects are much more difficult in shooting a pistol," Towsley says. "It's 10 times harder. It's a much bigger

commitment. Most guys can get a rifle to shoot, but you can't do that as easily with a handgun. Just like a rifle, you have to take a rest any time you can. A rifle is braced against you almost like a triangle. And that kind of locks it in fairly solidly compared to a handgun. A handgun is held out there away from your body. It's subject to all the little variances of trigger pull or a heartbeat. It's just not as solid."

"It changes the game," Weishuhn adds. "I'd love to shoot my .300 in Iowa, but part of the handgunning game comes in with the legal restrictions. And in certain instances hunting in thick cover (with a handgun) adds a different dimension to it. To me, I like to restrict myself to 60 yards when I'm hunting with a handgun. It's like bowhunting, but without quite the time commitment of having to shoot every day to practice."

Pistols chambered for rifle cartridges are another animal. With a good rest and good optic, 200- to 300-yard field accuracy is attainable. Thompson/Center Arms and Magnum Research offer some top-quality single-shot deer hunting pistols, while Savage and Weatherby have bolt-action models built for long-range work.

"I shoot them a lot, the T/C Contender and Encore and all the bolt guns," Towsley says. "I think the Encore is the gun for several factors. Versatility is one big factor because you can buy one gun and keep switching barrels. I like the 7mm-08 Rem., and my favorite scope for these guns is a 2.5-

8X Leupold. If there's an area where optics become a choice of ergonomics, it's in higher power handgun scopes."

Towsley and Weishuhn agree that these pistols still require a lot more shooting practice than the long guns. They say 200 to 300 yards is maximum range, depending on your abilities and the downrange energy of the particular load you're shooting. Again, consider the 1,000 foot-pound minimum.

MUZZLELOADERS

It's no wonder that so many gunmakers have jumped on the in-line muzzleloader bandwagon. Knight, Remington, Thompson/Center, Traditions and others have realized that deer hunters will take advantage of blackpowder deer seasons if they can find rifles that are easy to care for and shoot. In-line technology has made it so. With the cap in-line and right behind the powder charge, lock time is dramatically

reduced and so is the chance for a misfire. These guns also disassemble quickly and easily, making them less of a chore to clean than their predecessors.

In fact, in-line muzzleloading technology has made blackpowder the frequent choice over a slug gun when deer hunters have the option to use either.

"The slug guns that I've seen are fairly accurate, but a slug is not as efficient," says *North American Hunter* field editor Jim Shockey. "A slug dies badly after 125 yards, whereas a saboted muzzleloader bullet is still quite efficient out to 175 and even 200 yards. So, in the field a slug gun becomes a 75- to 100-

yard gun where a muzzleloader becomes a 100- to 130-yard gun. At those kinds of distances, how often do you need more than one shot?"

Of course, the slug gun hunter doesn't have to fret as much about inclement weather. Rain and snow cause many deer hunters to worry about whether or not a muzzleloader, even an in-line, will perform. Though they do require more care than a slug gun in wet weather, many hunters are amazed at how much moisture they can withstand. In fact, in one of the company's promotional videos, Tony Knight, originator of the Knight rifle, tosses one of his rifles into a pond, drags it out a few seconds later, caps it and then fires it without incident. The plastic sabot holding the bullet forms a tight seal around the powder charge. The weak link, as Shockey points out, is usually the cap.

"If you're going to have a misfire, it's not going to be because of the powder, it's going to be because of the cap," Shockey says. "As far as the weather goes, just change your caps (if they get wet). Of course, you can go to a Knight DISC rifle with the sealed shotgun primer and never have a problem."

No matter what modern muzzleloader you choose, selecting the right bullet is as critical as it is for slug gun hunters. Towsley says the all-copper models similar to those used in shotgun slugs are the best bet.

"When I started shooting the in-line muzzleloaders, the pistol bullets in sabots were a very poor choice." Towsley says. "We were driving them much faster than they ever were designed for. And I've seen the problems with on-game performance a number of times now. I was a huge fan of full-caliber conical bullets. But in my mind that all changed when Barnes brought out that copper bullet. These bullets are the bullet of choice today."

Today deer hunters have better choices all around when it comes to the other guns and ammunition. Tomorrow, somehow, the technology will get even better. But the bottom line is that deer hunting is what you make it. Though the guns might be capable of taking game cleanly at longer distances, you might be more satisfied by the accomplishment of taking deer at shorter ranges. That's the allure of some of these hunting tools and the deer hunting seasons that come with them.

Like shotguns, muzzleloaders have come a long way in the past decade. In-line ignition systems make these tools more reliable and incredibly accurate. And many states have special seasons just for blackpowder hunters to pursue whitetails.

BETTER BOWHUNTING

If you've read this far into this book, you should realize my passion for bowhunting for whitetails. It has been atop my list of hunting adventure since those early autumn days almost 20 years ago in east-central Wisconsin. I could devote a chapter, maybe an entire book, to why bowhunting has so captured my hunting spirit. But that won't necessarily help you hunt whitetails successfully. So let's stick to the point and try instead to take what I've learned and help you apply it in

the deer woods should you choose to go afield with an archery tag.

Some of you reading this are undoubtedly accomplished bowhunters in your own right; others might be a few years into the process and still searching for ways to improve. Still

others might hunt with rifles or muzzleloaders but have never tried the bow. To this last group, I say this: Bowhunting will make you a better deer hunter. I hunt with all manner of hunting tools when it comes to whitetails. And I enjoy each pursuit. But as sure as a buck uses his nose to search out danger, bowhunting teaches lessons about deer that you cannot learn during gun seasons. I say this with no notion that bowhunting makes me somehow better than those of you who do not bowhunt. I say it because I believe *that much* in the hours spent bowhunting. And because I love it so.

From bow stands I've seen about every deer behavior one might hope to witness. I've seen bucks dog does during the rut and battle other bucks for dominance. I've seen fawns suckle their mothers early in the season. I've had deer bust me with their eyes, ears and nose. I've had whitetails pass within five yards entirely oblivious to my presence. I've smelled the stench of rutting bucks and heard does, fawns and bucks vocalize in most every manner known.

Still, I'm sometimes surprised by what I witness in the whitetail woods during bow season. And thanks in large part to mountains of mistakes on my end and a few successes along the way, I've learned how to improve my odds. The nature of bowhunting is that you'll lose far more often than you'll win. But that's what keeps me coming back and makes me thankful for long seasons.

This section is going to focus mainly on gear, but in the sidebar called "The Little Things" (pages 148–149) you'll find a checklist of tactical information that I think is essential for any

Pope and Young would marvel at today's bowhunting equipment. Though those old-time archers might still choose their traditional gear, there is no arguing the performance of some of today's top compounds.

bowhunter hoping to attach his tag to a whitetail.

YOUR BOW

I've killed whitetails with a number of different compound bows, never with a recurve or longbow. If you hunt with a stick-bow, I'm not going to tell you anything you don't already know. And you're probably far enough along the bowhunting path that you don't need my help anyway. So, I'm going to stick to compounds, since that's what the vast majority of you will choose.

Improved Equipment

Bows have improved dramatically during the past two decades, so maybe I shouldn't be surprised if they get even better during the next 20 years. But I can't see much left to improve. Risers are machined from aluminum for light weight and strength. Single-cam bows have taken over the market with their smooth-shooting characteristics and stay-in-tune benefits. Strings and cables and limbs are more durable, and the entire modern compound bow is a more efficient machine that is more fun to shoot.

I'm not going to steer you to a particular brand of bow for your whitetail hunting. All the major manufacturers offer quality gear that will do the job. But I do suggest that if you're in the market for a bow, you concentrate your efforts on the single-cam models. Most every bowmaker has one, with good reason. It's just plain impossible to get a two-cam bow to perform as well as a quality single-cam. In fact, in talking to a lot of the bow manufacturers and veteran

Whether you shoot with fingers or a mechanical release aid doesn't matter. What does matter is that you practice as often as possible to prepare for that one important shot this season.

archers out there, I'd be surprised to see many two-cam bows being sold in the future.

More important than which make or model of bow you buy is how you set it up. Accessories like quivers, bow sights and stabilizers are just as critical to your deer hunting success as the bow itself. Your fully outfitted rig must be silent. If a whitetail hears your arrow shaft slide along the arrow rest or your quiver creak as you come to full draw, it won't matter a pinch if your souped up bow shoots 300 feet per second. You probably won't get a shot at all. And even if you do, a whitetail on full alert will jump the string and likely duck your arrow cleanly.

Rests & Other Details

Where the arrow meets the arrow rest is the downfall of most rigs when it comes to noise. If you use a mechanical release aid, as most bowhunters do, you probably are using a shoot-through style arrow rest, since an arrow released with a mechanical release tends to flex more up and down and requires, therefore, support below the arrow. Shoot-through style rests generally have two narrow prongs that cradle the arrow and slide between the fletching as the arrow is launched from the rest. If these prongs are metal on the type of rest you choose, they must be coated with a rubber shrink tube or Teflon sleeves available at any archery shop. Or you can often replace the metal prongs entirely with those made of Teflon or other quiet, durable material.

Arrow rests, like this Chuck Adams Super Slam rest designed for release aid shooters, must be whisper-quiet, rugged and easily adjustable. It is a critical link in your shooting and hunting success.

I'm entirely against wrapping metal prongs with moleskin or similar material. This stuff wears out quickly and changes shape dramatically when soaked by rain. These seemingly small changes can impact the angle of your arrow from bowstring to arrow rest, and, therefore, alter point of impact. This is especially true if you're shooting thin carbon shafts.

The downside of many of the shoot-through style rests is that they are relatively complex with a lot of moving parts, Allen screws and springs. If something goes haywire with your arrow rest, you're out of business until you can get it

fixed or replaced. Thus, I always choose the most simple, quality arrow rest I can find.

Well-known bowhunter Chuck Adams introduced a shoot-through arrow rest recently that looks very similar to a flipper rest design. If you take a flipper rest and stand it on end vertically, then add another flipper to form a "V"—that's the basic concept. Very few moving parts, simple, quiet, durable. I've had the good fortune to hunt whitetails with Chuck on a couple of occasions and know that he's a simplicity nut too. It shows in this arrow rest.

Quivers

Most bowhunters use a quiver that is attached to the bow. Tons of models are available, but cheap ones can wreck your hunt because they're noisy. If you use an attached quiver, make certain that it's silent. The only way to test that is to fill it full of arrows like you'll be using when you're hunting, and leave it on your bow whenever you shoot practice arrows.

Have someone go with you and stand close by to listen as you shoot. You might miss a small noise as you concentrate on the target. Your friend, though, might be able to detect a noise that could give you away to a deer. Because of the noise factor, many hunters, like Adams, choose a hip quiver or a detachable model that they remove from the bow and hang in the tree when they hunt.

Stabilizers & Silencers

Stabilizers absorb vibrations at the shot and help to further quiet your bow. Some models also help to balance the negative effects of torque and thereby improve accuracy. To me, a stabilizer is a matter of choice. You probably don't need it, since the accuracy difference is usually very small and most of your shots at whitetails are likely to be inside 25 yards. If your rig is noticeably quieter with a stabilizer, however, use one.

Same goes for string silencers like the rubber-cat-whisker types or the yarn "muffs." These usually take enough vibration out of the string to make a big difference in the noise factor. That's why most bowhunters will have some type of string silencer. Your archery pro shop expert will also be able to provide input on keeping your bow properly maintained and lubricated. Keeping your equipment in tiptop shape goes a long way toward avoiding problems during deer season.

ARROWS & BROADHEADS

Like bows, I've shot a variety of arrow shafts and broadheads. Before I get into the merits of these, the bottom line is this: Put a sharp broadhead in a whitetail's ribs at close range and you'll go home happy, regardless of what your arrows are made of or who manufactured that broadhead. If only it were that simple, right?

Choosing arrow shafts and broadheads is largely dependent on your bow setup, so your archery pro shop expert should play an important role in helping you make your choice.

Today's arrow shafts offer unmatched precision and toughness. An archery pro shop can help you select the right shaft size for your rig and tune your bow to shoot the shafts like darts.

Arrows

The first challenge will be getting an arrow shaft that will tune properly. Aluminum arrows are generally heavier than their carbon counterparts and, therefore, easier to get to group well with broadheads. I hate to generalize, but I'll say this: Most of you will be better off with aluminum shafts for your whitetail hunting. Despite what you might read about fast carbon arrows and flatter trajectories, it simply doesn't matter much once you go afield. Conditions in the deer woods are a lot different from at the bow range.

From a typical treestand in the woods, you might not be able to get a clear shot farther than 30 yards anyway. And if that's your maximum effective range, trajectory isn't much of an issue. Thus, a lighter shaft is no big advantage like it might be for a guy after antelope out West. According to statistics from the Pope and Young Club, the average shot distance for whitetail bucks entered in the record book is 18 yards.

Aluminum arrows, with full 5-inch helical fletches, will also steer broadheads more reliably too. I've shot thin carbon shafts with 4-inch offset vanes. I found broadheads that grouped well with these shafts, but the short fletch and lack of a helical twist made it more difficult to get broadheads flying consistently. A composite shaft like the Easton A/C/C, which has an aluminum core wrapped by carbon, is a good compromise if you're looking for lighter weight with good arrow flight. These are more expensive than an all-alu-minum shaft, but they are extremely durable and might be worth the extra initial investment.

Broadheads

As for broadheads, the key word is sharp. We ask a lot of a broadhead. Deer hair is hell on broadhead blades, then there's hide, bone and muscle. Like most things in life, you get what you pay for when it comes to broadheads. Demand that the blades are super sharp.

I'm not going to mention brands, but I will advise against choosing the expandable heads that have become relatively

Broadheads must be razor-sharp and bone-crushing tough. You must also find the right design and size so that your broadhead-tipped arrows fly true and group well.

popular. These heads feature blades that fold into the ferrule of the broadhead and open on impact. The concept is to offer a head that flies like a field point but delivers broad-head performance on impact. My recommendation against selecting these heads is based entirely on second-hand information. I've not tried them because I've heard too many bad things from bowhunters I respect. And I'm not going to try something that might cause me to lose an animal just to say I tried it.

The manufacturers of expandable broadheads admit that penetration is reduced with this design. They also admit that the open-on-impact engineering means that you need an arrow delivering a lot more energy than you would if you were using a fixed blade design. Angling shots and impact with bone raise other potential problems for the expand-ables. This is a point that cannot be argued: all else being equal, a quality fixed blade head will perform better on game than an expandable. Those who choose expandables usually do so because they shoot bows that are extremely fast or not properly tuned and, therefore, won't group fixed-blade broadheads. These speed rigs often feature overdraw arrow rest setups, light carbon shafts and high-draw-weight two-cam bows. You will do much better with a slow bow, a heavy arrow and big, shaving-sharp, fixed blade broadhead from the average treestand whitetail hunting setup.

CLOTHING & HIDING

Like your bow, bowhunting clothing better be quiet. If you scratch your bowhunting clothing with your fingernails and hear noise, buy some new stuff.

Without getting into arguments about the merits of warmth, breathability or water-resistance, fleece and wool are still the best fabrics for bowhunters. The upper body layers must fit well, so as not to get in the way when trying to draw or release the bowstring. A full-length armguard and chest protector are valuable gear that I always recommend if you're wearing more than a couple of layers of clothing. You don't want to have to think about keeping your clothes out of the way when you're trying to get in position and aim.

I see some bowhunters wearing camo face masks and like the idea of hiding a shiny face from the eyes of a whitetail, but I can't stand face masks when I'm bowhunting. They don't ever fit me right and always seem to be in the way. So, when I think I need to, I smear on a bunch of camo makeup to hide my face. I've killed deer without wearing any camo on my

Will your bow perform when the weather is at its worst? Test draw your bow in cold weather and wet weather to see if it's making any noises that could spook an approaching buck.

If you bowhunt from a treestand, you must wear a safety belt or harness. Many deer hunters are seriously injured each year in falls from treestands.

face, but I'm generally paranoid about such matters, so I usually cover up whenever possible.

Most bowhunters wear knee-high rubber boots of some type until later in the year up North, when those are replaced with warmer pac boots. Rubber boots make sense since they don't hold odors or give away your foot scent to approaching deer. However, rubber likes to squeak against metal treestand platforms. And I've had more than one whitetail make me as I was trying to twist a foot into comfortable shooting position. Some bowhunters use a carpet mat on the platform.

I'm going to go to some of the stalker-type booties made to fit over your boots. These are available from the mail-order places like Cabela's and are generally intended to help hunters stalk close to game. But I figure they also ought to work well in a treestand. The other thing about rubber boots is that they don't breath and, therefore, they cause feet to sweat more. So use scent-destroying powder inside your boots after every hunt then store them in sealed containers, just like you should do with your hunting clothing. You have to think head-to-toe for whitetails.

Think Safety Too

One more item that kind of falls under the clothing realm is a safety harness. I've always known the importance of strapping myself to the tree when hunting from an elevated stand. But it took the birth of my first child, Ben, to really make me stop and think. No whitetail is worth a fall from one of the high hunting stands that I like. A good safety harness is better than a simple waist belt. The fact that it goes over the shoulders and across the waist also helps pull in

clothing, which keeps it out of the way for drawing and shooting your bow. Again, think about the noise factor when you look over various models of safety gear. Hunting whitetails at close range with archery equipment is an incredible challenge. Proof is in the fact that success rates for bowhunters in most states are somewhere around just 25 percent despite incredibly long seasons. If you want to be one of the minority of successful hunters, pay attention to all the little things with your gear this coming bow season.

A pull-up rope seems like an obvious piece of gear, but some hunters still try to climb with a bow or gun in hand. That's too dangerous. Having all the necessary items makes your hunting more enjoyable and productive.

The Little Things

If you've paid attention to all of the points in the main section, bowhunting now comes down to the little things.

I put moleskin on the bow's riser and on the shelf of my arrow rest in case the arrow somehow falls from the rest while I'm in my stand. Nothing like an aluminum-to-aluminum "clink" to steer a whitetail away from your tree. I also draw the bow a couple of times each time I get into my stand. Sometimes a small twig, piece of mud, frost or ice not noticed after the previous hunt can cause a noise the

first time you draw on your next hunt. I don't want that to be when I'm taking aim at a deer. A couple of test draws help to loosen your muscles too.

Rangefinding: You have an advantage when you wait for whitetails in a stand. You know where to expect them to show up. That means you can know the yardages before the deer arrive on the scene. Some hunters pace off distances to their tree and use natural markers as reminders so that they don't have to estimate the range by eye when a whitetail appears. I carry a laser rangefinder

Draw weight: I know guys who drive jacked-up four-wheel-drive trucks with modified exhaust systems and big tires. These are the same types who think they need an 80-pound bow to get the job done on deer. I shoot 60 pounds and can't see a reason for anything more than that on a whitetail. More draw weight often means more noise. I used to watch a guy at the bow range who shot an 80-pound bow. It cracked like a .22 rifle when he shot it. Slow-motion video proves that an alert whitetail is faster than any arrow, so the argument that speed counters noise is bunk. Less draw weight has other advantages. It's easier to draw slowly, smoothly, hold longer and aim more solidly. And then it does the job with quiet precision. Bowhunting is not a muscle game; it's all finesse.

On the ground: Though we talk about bowhunting whitetails and treestands hand in hand, there are times when a ground blind is the only way to go. Some of this is mentioned in the "Taking A Stand" section in Chapter 4. I've seen situations where a good buck is vulnerable only in a place where there's no good tree for a stand. Don't shy away from hunting on the ground with a bow. Many deer are killed every year by bowhunters on the ground. Use the natural surrounding cover to your advantage or check out

one of the commercially available portable blinds with shoot-through windows. Just make sure you give yourself a comfortable seat and that you can draw and shoot without having to shift positions. At eye level, movement is a killer. And you aren't going to catch any breaks with your scent going over a close-range whitetail's head. Less room for error, but sometimes your only option. Get the wind right, then be a statue, and you can kill a whitetail from the ground.

Bowhunters should not forsake the ground. Even though the vast majority of whitetails are taken by treestand hunters, some setups call for a ground stand.

and use it each time I hunt a new treestand. I quickly zap surrounding trees or other objects so that I know yardages to the various spots where I might get a shot. That's one less worry when a whitetail comes slinking into range.

Bow hangers: I like to hold my bow in my hands while I hunt, but many bowhunters use screw-in bow hangers and hang their bow against the tree within arm's reach. There are some advantages to this. You can sit more still without having to monkey with a bow in your hands. Hanging the bow also means less hand and arm fatigue; and fatigued muscles don't perform as well as rested ones when it comes time to shoot.

THE DEER HUNTER'S DAYPACK

nce upon a time I went deer hunting with my coat and pant pockets filled with compasses, snacks, rope, handwarmers and all the other "stuff" I might need for the day. What a sight! It's difficult enough to kill a whitetail, why compound the challenge by being unorganized?

Every deer hunter should carry a daypack on his back. A small backpack is a critical piece of gear that helps ensure that you'll have what you need when you need it. And it's really the only reasonable way to get all of your gear out there comfortably and conveniently.

If you're like me and prefer to have everything "with you," you'll want to invest in a good-sized pack with wide shoulder straps and a waist belt. You'll also want a daypack that is water-resistant to protect the contents. Most daypacks are so designed and will protect the contents unless you really get soaked.

Some high-quality daypacks offer an internal frame that provides support and distributes weight more evenly. If you'll be hiking in very hilly country like in the Adirondacks or some Western whitetail habitat, these higher-end packs are a good choice. Fanny packs are also relatively popular for this purpose, but I dislike them compared to daypacks. They generally won't carry as much equipment and don't ride as comfortably as a daypack with shoulder straps.

As I've preached throughout this book, all of your gear must be chosen with the noise factor in mind. Select fleece backpacks. Also check out the zippers before you buy. Some are very loud. Find those that open and close with a whisper. A topnotch daypack is a solid investment that you'll be happy to have.

A daypack allows you to carry necessary gear in comfort. That way you won't have to leave the woods for a snack or to go get your knife after your deer is down.

PACKING YOUR PACK—THE NECESSITIES

Some items always go with me. I'll start with the necessities for any deer hunter's daypack.

Fire-starting kit: Whether it's waterproof matches, a butane lighter or some other form of fire-starter, you better have it. When you need it, you really need it. It doesn't matter if you're only hunting a couple of hundred yards from the truck. The Boy Scout motto, "Be prepared" applies all the time. A fire can save your life; a lot of lost souls have found that out over the years.

Compass & map of the area: Same concept applies here. But some of you surely know every square inch of the "Back 40" where you deer hunt. For you folks, okay, I'll admit that you need not carry a compass. If you are not intimately familiar with the country, however, you must have a compass

and map and know how to use them. Always tell a friend or family member where you'll be hunting in case you get lost or injured.

Rope: Whether it's to pull your gun or bow up into your treestand or to tie branches together for an overnight shelter, 25 to 30 feet of thin rope is another item you'll always find in my pack.

Knife & sharpener: Best case scenario, you'll need it to field dress your deer. Worst case, well, a knife comes in handy for many jobs. Some deer hunters choose to wear their knife on their belt so that it's always within reach. This is a good idea, provided it's a folding model or safely tucked into a sturdy sheath.

Safety harness: If you'll be hunting from a treestand, you must have a safety harness. As soon as you get in your treestand you must attach yourself securely, before you pull

Binoculars are an item that should always have a place in your daypack. Picking out deer from a distance gives you time to get into position for a shot without alerting the animals.

for most whitetail hunting applications. Mini binoculars don't gather light well enough for my liking early and late in the day when deer are often on the move. So, despite their compact size advantage, I generally don't hunt with them.

I've also come to rely heavily on a laser rangefinder especially when I'm bowhunting. If you're hunting with a rifle in a wooded setting you might not have shooting beyond 100 yards anyway, so a laser rangefinder isn't an important tool. But if you're after Western whitetails in more open country where shots can extend to 200 yards and farther, you'll be way ahead of the game knowing the distance to the yard. When bowhunting, the laser rangefinder gives me exact distances to surrounding reference points so that I don't have to try to guess by eye when I'm trying to concentrate on drawing my bow and picking a spot.

Multi-tool: Another one that could easily fall under the mandatory list. It's no wonder these excellent devices have become so popular that just about every major knife maker has a multi-tool of its own. I've used the screwdriver heads to tighten a quiver bracket and the saw blade to cut small branches that blocked shooting lanes.

Chemical handwarmers: These small packets help me hunt longer than I could without them. I'll admit, my hands have been frozen too many times while ice fishing; I'm a wimp when it comes to cold fingers. Numb fingers don't do well when it comes to shooting a bow or working a safety on my deer rifle. If it's going to be colder than 40°F, I have handwarmers with me.

Umbrella: You've probably seen the compact umbrellas that attach to the tree trunk above your stand. These fold to the size of a set of small shooting sticks about 12 inches long and a few inches in diameter. They attach in minutes to the tree and fold out wide enough to give you a full roof and keep you dry when it starts to rain or snow. Not only does this keep you warmer, but it keeps moisture out of your riflescope and off your feather-fletched arrows.

Grunt calls, rattle box, deer lure: Depending on the situation I might tuck a call or rattling device into my daypack. If the rut is near, I always have a grunt tube with me. Some bucks that would have otherwise simply gone about their business out of range have come close enough to kill thanks to a grunt tube. Same for the rattle box. And I've had enough good experiences with deer lures, that I often have a bottle in my daypack.

Wind detector: Though I know which way the wind is blowing before I ever get to my stand, I like having a small plastic puff bottle along to check the air currents as the day

up the rest of your gear or do anything else. Too many people are permanently crippled and killed every year in falls from treestands.

Headlamp and spare batteries: Flashlights are fine, but I much prefer the hands-free utility of a headlamp when it comes to finding my way into my stand or blood-trailing a buck. The multi-directional beam adjustment means that I also can set the lamp on the ground and aim wherever I need light.

Pee bottle and toilet paper: Enough said.

NOT NECESSARY, BUT NICE

Snacks and drinking water: I like to carry Nutri-Grain or PowerBars if I'm going to be hunting all day. Some guys need more food to get through an entire day on stand, especially in really cold weather. But I'm always stingy on space in my daypack and don't like a bunch of sandwiches or a Thermos taking up a lot of room. For all-day sits I'll also carry a 16-ounce plastic water bottle with a double cap to ensure against water leaking inside my pack.

Optics: I almost always include these under the necessary list because they really are. I hate being caught in a deer stand without binoculars. A hunter armed with good optics sees more game and saves time trying to assess whether or not the animal is one that he wants to shoot. And, especially when it comes to mature bucks, every second counts.

Mid-sized binoculars in the 7-power range are about right

progresses. A baby powder bottle with seven or eight small holes in the top and filled with foot powder sends out a nice cloud that you can easily track as it wafts away. This will let you know where deer are likely to get your wind and helps you plan when and where you'll need to shoot a deer in order to avoid being smelled first.

Camera: I like in-the-field photos of deer right where it actually happened. Carrying a small camera in a zip-top bag allows me to do this. Disposable cameras work great too.

Unscented bow or gun lube: Nothing's worse than a squeaky treestand seat or an arrow rest that is suddenly making noise. Murphy's Law will surely come into play if you're not prepared. And then when it finally does happen, you can silence the noisemaker on the spot. A tiny 1-ounce bottle of bow lube like the Tetra Bow Lube that I carry works great.

Screw-in bow hangers: Even for rifle hunters these are handy. I use them to hang up my rangefinder, binoculars, grunt call and the daypack itself. This keeps these items within arm's reach but out of the way when I have to position for a shot.

Reflective tacks or flagging: If you shoot a deer and leave to get help to track it, reflective tacks or surveyor's tape should be used to mark the spot where you last saw the deer. This will make it easier to pick up the trail. You can also use these items to mark a new scrape or rub that you want to check the next day. Just make sure to clean up these items when you're done hunting this location.

Packing for a day with the deer requires a lot of planning. The more you hunt, the more you'll learn about which items you just have to have in your daypack in order to successfully hunt whitetails.

Hang everything within arm's reach, but out of the way. This hunter is settling in for an all-day sit.

Chapter 6

WHY I DEER HUNT

I would have been easy to give up on whitetail hunting all those years ago, but I guess what I lacked in deer hunting knowledge I made up for in determination.

There was that autumn night I slept in Paul Weber's cabin. I might have been 14 or 15 and had not yet taken a deer. Early in the morning, Paul, a friend of my father's, walked me out to a place by a wide oak where I waited with my bow for daylight. Paul circled back the way we had come and at first light made a gentle push that he hoped would send a deer toward my stand. And, sure enough, an hour or so after light a young 6-point buck trotted through the frosty fall leaves and stopped not 15 yards behind my tree. I got myself turned around in time, had an arrow ready on the string, but never drew my bow as the deer walked slowly, stiff-legged out of sight over the ridge. Buck fever had a stranglehold on me that wonderful morning, and deer hunting has never loosened its grip on my soul.

Whitetail hunting has taken me from Idaho to Louisiana and most points in between. I've taken some record-class deer, and I've killed does that have made me proud. I've shared deer camps with men, women and children with whitetail-hunting history pumping through their veins. They are all, like me, helpless, really, when it comes to whitetails.

Once during my travels, a woman from Philadelphia sat next to me on a plane and noticed an article of my clothing that advertised my passion for hunting. Without much warning, she challenged my morality. She was an anti-hunter and couldn't understand how I could kill "defenseless deer."

I'd like to tell you how I eloquently argued her into submission with airtight logic for hunting. But, in reality, I listened mostly as she ranted and raved about the wild creatures she proclaimed to love. In her mind I was a barbarian, and she, of lofty intelligence, had evolved to possess some higher moral sensibilities than her ancestors, who relied on wild animals for survival.

As we deplaned I'm certain that she left quite full of herself and more convinced of her own beliefs. I hadn't argued at all. I hadn't agreed either, of course, but I chose to listen to her perspectives rather than get into a discussion that never would have been resolved to either party's satisfaction during a two-hour flight.

I had taken the same approach during a discussion in an environmental ethics philosophy course at the University of Wisconsin-Madison where I eventually earned my degree in journalism. I knew without asking that I was the only hunter in the discussion group of 30 or more students. It also was clear that the professor had never fired a deer rifle or fried venison tenderloins for dinner. We spent that one day of an entire semester talking about hunting.

One day. That was it. With little debate everyone else in the room concluded that hunting was a silly, antiquated pursuit, not necessary, in fact detrimental, to the well-being of the environment. I apologize to all of you for not standing up to fight. At 20, I wasn't prepared to do much to help protect the hunting tradition. Today I wish that I could go back for a couple of hours to that environmental ethics discussion and to that flight next to the lady from Philadelphia.

Deer hunting is not something I choose, it chooses me. I believe this with every single fiber of my being. My best friend and brother-in-law, Mike Vogel, and I used to traipse around Wisconsin together. Sometimes a boat trailed behind as we aimed for a muskie lake; other times the pickup bed was packed with sleeping bags and bows en route to the northern forest. This happened most every weekend for some years, and we talked a lot about why we were going to cast bucktails in the rain or sleep in the back of a pickup on a 10-degree night during deer season while our classmates and the young ladies of our affection socialized at parties.

You know what? We thought that *they* were all entirely crazy. We could not imagine life any different from what we were making of it. We missed weddings of close relatives, we skipped school together, we got into a heap of trouble because we were always late coming home, but we were helpless when it came to hunting and fishing.

There was that one October afternoon when Mike had come down with mononucleosis. (Okay, we found a little time during the week to smooch with the girls.) But it was duck season, and the marsh was calling. I knew that Mike was sick, but I paced his parents' home knowing that he'd snap out of it. He'd tough it out. And a couple of hours later he was push-poling our skiff through the cattails, and I was shooting mallards as they jumped from the secluded backwaters. Mike shouldn't have been out there; I shouldn't have asked him, but I couldn't help it.

I was born this way. The woman from Philadelphia and my

environmental ethics classmates might say that so goes the argument of axe murderers and other deviants. To that I say that those people without the passion or appreciation for the hunt flowing through their veins have deviated from the way God intended.

I don't say that non-hunters are bad people. My wife is a non-hunter. But she appreciates my motivation to hunt. I contend that hunters act on an instinct that for thousands of years accounted for man's very survival. I ask how I should be able to act differently when all of those generations of ancestors were hunters. How can I not hunt? And how in the world can anyone, no matter what our landscape looks like today, say that hunting is wrong?

Take the wolf and fence him in. Feed him more elk and deer meat than he could ever hope to hunt down in the wild. Is it a better thing that the wolf shouldn't have to act so savagely and rip out the throat of a flailing elk in order to feed itself and the rest of the pack? Has that wolf attained some higher moral sensibility? What is a wolf if he doesn't hunt? I say he's no longer a wolf. I can buy beef at the market less than a mile from my house. I can be

entertained at ball games. But, like the wolf, I am not whole without hunting.

The deer woods make me whole. When I breathe the heavy, cold November cedar air, I breathe the same air that caused my ancestors' muscles to tense and eyes to strain through the forest. And when I eat the flesh of a whitetail, I taste life and death. All of this is not without its ironies. I care deeply for the animals I hunt.

Once in high school I was driving home from a late wrestling practice. And from a dark ditch on that country road I glimpsed a white-tailed doe just before it ran headlong into the side of my car with incredible force. Turning around a couple of hundred yards farther down the road, I saw the deer lying on the centerline, head up and still alive. I drove up within 10 yards or so, kept the headlights on her and got out of the car. There was nothing I could do, but I wanted to be sure that if she was mortally injured that she not suffer. As I stood at arm's length, I decided to try to help her to her feet. And without much struggle she finally stood, still close enough to touch and still dazed, I'm sure, from the impact. As she gathered her senses, she focused on me, stared for a few moments, recognized me as a human predator and then dashed back into the woods.

I know other hunters who have bellycrawled across thin ice to rescue deer that have fallen into rivers or lakes. And I've heard anti-hunters say that these efforts are not at all about any affection for these animals, but rather, some selfish effort to ensure that we heartless hunters have deer to blast come fall. That, they say, is also the motivation for all of the millions of dollars that hunters dedicate toward conservation.

To these dim views I can say only this: The fact that deer still live in the same woods where I first hunted two decades ago is important to me, not so that I can return to kill another whitetail there someday, but rather that I can take my son there. Maybe someday my grandson or granddaughter. Maybe one of them will kill a deer in that woods and maybe not. I simply want there to be hunting grounds for the generations of Gutschows to follow me. I want white-tailed deer to appear in their dreams, tense their muscles and shake their nerves. That way, like me, they'll know that they truly are alive.

My father has a habit of calling me weeks before the Wisconsin deer season is set to open. Outside of deer

season we might talk on the phone every couple of weeks. But during the final two weeks before opening day, we talk just about every day. Sure, there are reasons for these calls, "Don't forget to bring an extra gallon of milk," or "I picked up a new knife sharpening kit we'll have to try out." But these are excuses to call because we don't know what else to do with ourselves.

Dad doesn't get too excited about anything except deer hunting. He fishes in summer and hunts for wild turkeys in spring and grouse in October, but doesn't care much if he's out at the crack of dawn or not. Deer hunting is different. He changes his mind about his Opening Day stand location five times in the two weeks before opener. He makes lists of things that he's packed every year for three decades of deer hunting. He sights-in the old .30-06 that shoots just the same as it did last year. And every year he tries to get to the deer hunting cabin a day earlier and stay a day longer.

My son, Ben, was in the backseat of Grandpa's car and still not a year old when he saw his first live, wild whitetails up close. My parents and my wife and I were driving slowly through the summer woods of a state park in Door County, Wisconsin, early in the evening. A doe in her reddish-brown summer coat stood 15 yards off the road in stark contrast to the lush green foliage surrounding her. Dad slowed the car to a stop, and she stayed put. There had

to be fawns close by, and before long I had the twins spotted as they moved closer to their mother. Ben, by now, had been lifted from his car seat to get a clear view out the side window. His eyes found the flicking ears and tails quickly and he pointed and belted out "dee, dee, dee," just as he had when I first explained that the animal heads on the wall of our home were called "deer." Ben was more excited than if he'd been handed a bottle of warm milk. And his eyes remained fixed on the whitetails until they evaporated into the summer woods.

Deer hunting needs no defense. It is in my father's blood. It is in my blood. It is in my son's blood. It just is, and may it always be so.

INDEX